JOB HUNTING
FOR THE 40+ EXECUTIVE

JOB HUNTING
FOR THE 40+ EXECUTIVE

E. Patricia Birsner

Facts On File Publications
New York, New York ● Oxford, England

JOB HUNTING FOR THE 40+ EXECUTIVE

Library of Congress Cataloging in Publication Data

Birsner, E. Patricia.
   Job hunting for the 40+ executive.

   Includes index.
   1. Executives—United States. 2. Age and
employment—United States. 3. Job hunting—United
States. I. Title.
HF5500.3.U54B57   1984   650.1'4'024658   83-18489
ISBN 0-87196-634-4

Composition by Facts On File/Circle Graphics
Printed in the United States of America
10   9   8   7   6   5   4   3   2   1

Contents

Introduction

Middle-Aged and Out of Work

So, here you are. Middle-aged (or older) and out of work, perhaps for the first time in your life. How could this happen to you?

For many reasons, of course. The general economy may explain your out-of-work status. Or, a downturn in sales in your own particular industry or company necessitated a reduction in force, a layoff, a job reclassification or job change in which your former job disappeared. Your company or division may have closed or gone bankrupt. Or funding for your job or organization disappeared, which happens so often in the nonprofit or governmental sectors. All of these are valid, understandable reasons. But you still feel bad—and you're still unemployed.

You begin your job search. To your horror, you find myriad employment problems directly related to your years, a set of nebulously stated but very real prejudices against hiring older executives.

In the depression of the 1930s, these prejudices seemed to be directed against anyone over 40. In the 1980s, the age barrier has moved upward closer to the 50-year mark. American executives today are health- and appearance-conscious. They take better care of themselves than in earlier times. The average life span has increased from 62 in 1938 to around 76 for men and from 65 to 82 for women. But because executive and professional people do take better care of themselves, they live even longer. Therefore, if you're 50 to 55, you can anticipate living 28 more years; if you're 55 to 60, expect another 24; if you're 60 to 65, that translates to around 20 additional years to work and live. The perception of what is middle-age and what is old age has moved because life expectancy has increased.

But many of the perceptions of business about the older executive remain unchanged, even though the threshold has moved upward. Conventional (but faulty) hiring wisdom says:

- Older executives are more expensive to hire.
- Older executives have reduced capabilities. They are slower, take longer to complete tasks and make more errors. They don't have the energy needed to do the job. Therefore, they are not cost effective, given their salary scales.
- Older executives haven't kept up with the changes in the work world. Their skills are obsolete. (Think about this: Did you perhaps lose your job because your superiors felt you had failed to stay current? Did you believe those computers would never be able to do the work you could do—or did you refuse to learn how to use them?)
- Older executives will be a drain on the pension plan since they will only work 10 or 15 years before retiring.
- Older executives cost more for medical, life insurance and other benefits.
- Something must be wrong with out-of-work older executives because they were let go by their former employers. (This reason, however, is not exclusive to age; the young unemployed executive faces the same prejudice.)
- Conversely, the older executive is overqualified for the position and won't stay if hired.
- Older executives don't have recent "hands-on" experience since they've spent most of their recent work experience managing or supervising rather than doing.
- Older executives don't have the adaptability or the necessary background for the job. Because the older executive has not had the specific background called for in the job specification, he or she cannot fill the position. While this prejudice is not age specific, the ramifications for the older manager are more subtle. A company will take a chance that a younger applicant

can remedy any deficits in experience while assuming that the older applicant can't learn quickly and will take too long to train and bring "up to speed."

□ Older executives will not be as loyal to the company as a younger person who can be brought along in "company style."

□ Older executives offer less opportunity to fill compliance guidelines.

□ Companies can hire a younger minority executive who will work for less money and at the same time help the company comply with EEO requirements.

The same age prejudices are faced by both male and female executives. But a woman manager has to contend additionally with some residue of prejudice against hiring females for executive positions. The female in a profession probably faces less hiring prejudice, unless she wishes to go into the management ranks. But to have made it into the executive category at all, the older female executive has had to be aggressive, assertive and tough. These very qualities which helped her make it before can now get in the way unless they are handled properly.

You want to work, you know you can work and do a job for someone. As an older unemployed executive, what will you face during this period of unemployment? What can you do to improve your chances of getting exactly the right position? And how can you counter the subtle and not so subtle ageism prejudices? Read on. Some of the hints will perhaps be things you already know. Others will be things you've forgotten. And some of the advice will be different from when you entered the job market or from conventional wisdom of a few years ago. But it doesn't hurt to review.

Emotional Traumas

The emotional traumas of the unemployed executive or professional job-seeker are the biggest single difference between the employed and the unemployed searcher. These traumas must be dealt with if your story is to have a happy ending.

Your feelings may run the entire emotional gamut. Some of you are angry. Your company (or bosses) are bloodsuckers. They (or he or she) were unfair, dictatorial, unfeeling. Or you may be directing your anger inward. "You dummy! How could you be so stupid!" You may direct your anger at society in general. "The damn government!" (Or the President, Congress, Democrats, Republicans, whatever.) Often, you turn your anger on family members—a spouse or children. You may feel vindictive, have a strong desire to "get even." (God forbid that you should act on this!)

Others of you are defeated. You feel destroyed, degraded, a total failure. You are demoralized. You've lost confidence in yourself, in your ability to do a good job, to support your family, even to look successfully for another job. (This also applies to unemployed older women executives, many of whom are divorced, widowed or the sole support of their families.) You show these feelings through your very appearance, posture, dress.

You may blame yourself. "It's all my fault—if I'd done such and such differently, if I'd just seen what was going on." You feel guilty of some transgression—real or imagined. You are embarrassed because of your "inadequacies."

You may blame others for your unemployment. The fault was your boss's, the personnel manager's, another manager's (the so-and-so was just out to get me). The feelings may be of disbelief. You are incredulous that this is happening to you. You went to the right schools, belonged to the right clubs, went to the right church or synagogue, and played the game of politics well (you thought). You've led a charmed life, so this can't be happening to you. (But there you are, still out on the street!)

In addition, you may be anxious and confused. "What am I going to do? How will I find a job? What's going to happen to me, my family? Am I obsolete? An anachronism? Should I change careers?" And on and on. You may be in such a state of panic that you feel immobilized, unable to take action on your own behalf.

How about hurt and indignation? Frustration? Depression? Rejection and pain? Yes, these are also common reactions. In fact, the middle aged, recently unemployed may feel so much pain that they suffer heart attacks, strokes or develop a panoply of psychosomatic illnesses which they must overcome in addition to the basic necessity of finding work. And frustration and depression unfortunately are ongoing problems throughout the job search.

If your entire working career (twenty years or more) was spent with one company, your reactions may be closer to those suffered by the "wronged" party in a particularly messy divorce or to those caused by the death of a loved one. Did you dedicate yourself to pleasing "the company?" Did it serve as wife, husband, mistress, lover? If so, you may feel bitter, spurned. Or the pain on separation may be a huge emptiness, a void. You want (and probably need) time to grieve.

What about your reactions? Did you experience any of the above emotions? They represent normal human responses to traumatic events.

And through all of this runs the nagging doubt that just maybe your problems are related to your age. If you were just younger, you wouldn't have been singled out—you would still be working.

Problems Can Increase as the Job Search Lengthens

Your initial emotional responses may be replaced by other more damaging ones as the time allocated to your job search lengthens. For currently unemployed middle-aged executives, the average time without work is almost eight months. (This time frame is longer than that of younger unemployed executives.) But this varies from just a few weeks to the almost chronic state of 18 months or more. And the longer the time frame, the more difficult and intransigent the emotional upset.

As an unemployed person, you tend to be at loose ends. You may not know what to do with yourself. Don't foolishly settle for the television set, the daily soap opera, the living room couch. To quote one such person, "my brain turned into silly putty on a steady diet of the boob tube." This can happen if you do not reset your goals (too often determined solely by your work) and don't develop a plan of action to keep going and growing.

You may feel friendless, isolated and lost. Listen to one unemployed female executive (age 48): "My existing friends didn't want to hear about my problems because they were too close to their own fears." Another woman (45): "I've always had a lot of social friends. A few of these came through beautifully, others didn't at all." A severe reaction from a long-term unemployed male (55): "I never developed any relationships or friendships. I had nothing to fall back on, to add to my feelings of self-worth." One former long-term friend abandoned an out-of-work executive for another reason: "I got so tired listening to that guy tell me about his troubles. All he did was bitch and gripe about what a raw deal he got . . . I couldn't see that he was doing one constructive thing to get his life back together. So, I just quit returning his phone calls and avoided places where I thought I might bump into him." And finally, you may simply not want to burden your friends with your troubles. So *you* may be the person who is doing the abandoning, losing a real source of support and even a long-term friendship in the bargain.

Have you gotten your anger under control so you can use that energy in your job search? Or do you still have it, lashing out at others when you least expect it? Your family and friends end up bearing the brunt of it. And, it could show up unexpectedly in the middle of that sometime thing, the interview.

You may also lose confidence to the point where you aren't sure you can do anything that anyone or any company would pay for. You may have trouble writing a resumé, answering ads or making calls on potential employers.

Your anxiety level may rise. And fear can enter the picture, too. Older executives have high life styles—high in fixed expenses, loan payments, running costs. You may have been keeping up with your neighbors. Suddenly your income is a tiny unemployment payment and your minimum requirements are in excess of $3,000 per month—and that's before you even eat! Perhaps you didn't make initial expenditure cuts, thinking your severance pay would be enough to tide you over without affecting your family during the short time you would be unemployed.

Even mundane expenditures become major considerations and many are unable to cope. As one sixtyish executive explained: "Older executives like me were brought up during the depression. Bankruptcy or failure to meet one's obligations was presented to us as an absolute disgrace. Being out of work for a long time can negate all our background and destroy the actual core of our belief in ourselves. It may ruin our ethical and moral fiber. I feel like I have a runaway reactor inside me involved in a self-destructive chain reaction."

As the time lengthens, divorce may become a real likelihood. Wives or husbands may become so disillusioned with their spouses that they file for divorce (or actually go through with the divorce). This is especially true for nonworking wives. The firing or job loss, coupled with the spouse's inability to get a better job immediately, has removed their "white knight" from his horse. They see their husbands as losers and they want to cut their losses. Men with executive wives may hear suggestions that they do a role reversal; i.e., stay home and be "househusbands." And the female executive may be given the "why don't you just stay home now and be a housewife" comment once too often.

Both men and women may lose their interest in sex. Men see this as additional confirmation that they are too old and "out-of-it." Their wives try to be supportive, but when they are turned away or not sought out in bed, they believe their husbands are indifferent or are freezing them out. The related experience of the unemployed older female executive is equally debilitating. They feel unlovable, unfeminine and unattractive. Since this may be occurring at about the same time as the menopause, they may see the loss as an inescapable part of that natural event. Their husbands may receive entirely too many "I don't feel like it tonight" or "I've got a headache" responses. And since sex is not a comfortable subject for discussion in this age group, the very real problems are not aired and may simply fester and add to the overall problem situation.

Loss of sexual response, though, is a very common part of clinical depression. It occurs often enough to be one of depression's major symptoms. And depression is concomitant with unemployment too often to be safely ignored.

If you don't lose your sex drive, something equally dangerous to the health of your marriage may occur. Either the unemployed male or female, in a frantic attempt to shore up self-esteem, may indulge in an affair or series of affairs, completing the tearing of the marriage fabric. And if it was the first time in a long and good marriage, should the actual affair not destroy you, the guilt may.

Take action before you lose it all.

Don't Add to Your Problems

You can damage yourself in other, more deliberate ways. You can involve yourself in any of the following self-destructive and self-fulfilling prophecies.

▢ Are you a social drinker? It's very easy to stop at the nearest bar earlier in the day for a pick-me-up. After all, you need it. Or you may start patronizing places you would never normally visit, and begin your serious drinking at noon. You end up with two problems instead of one. It's far too easy to crawl into the bottle as an escape from the grim realities "out there." And if you were already a heavy drinker, these behaviors may be just enough to push you over the line into alcoholism.

▢ Cursed with anxiety? How about a few tranquilizers, uppers, etc., from your obliging doctor—or worse yet—your local purveyor of chemical pleasures? Another vicious cycle. You take the drug to reduce anxiety and tension before an interview, for example. If one is good, maybe two will be better. Then, you are too loose and not quite together during the interview and you blow it. You hate yourself and become anxious all over again. You take another drug to feel better. Round and round it goes. The first thing you know, you have a dependency. And both alcohol and drugs further depress the already clinically depressed individual.

▢ Tired of the rat race? Just drop out. Quit caring for your appearance. Don't shave or wash your hair. If you're a female manager, quit wearing makeup and going to the beautician. Wear sloppy, casual wear or unpressed suits. Absolutely no one will hire you for the kind of executive or professional jobs you formerly held. You don't look the part. You'll have to settle for a more menial position because that's the way you are presenting yourself.

▢ Doing some wishful thinking? If you just wish long enough and hard enough, a job will come out of the woodwork without your having to do anything. (Not likely!) Be defensive—take offense at everything—"you're always criticizing me," "they're just picky," "that wasn't what I meant." This also is defeating and guaranteed to make the job search longer, more difficult and less likely to be successful. And the most serious emotional problem of all—the self-destructive urge to end it all, to commit suicide.

▫ Are these concerns exaggerated and blown up? Unfortunately, no. And this is where you come in. By consciously planning and working toward a goal, by seeking help when you need it, you can lessen the likelihood that you will fall prey to these disasters. Even if you are reading this book late in the job search and are already a victim, you may find some ways to extricate yourself from the morass.

How Do Reactions Differ?

Your sex and marital status are related to some other major differences affecting your interior emotional climate. The situations are different between male and female, and among the single, divorced and married executives. These differences need to be considered.

Male executives are mostly married, although many find themselves without support from their wives and families. Their wives may also feel demoralized and defeated and be unable to provide support. In many ways, married executives whose wives don't work have the toughest time. They have to be strong because of the very people depending upon them. They can't give way—they are expected to perform. They aren't even allowed to be sad, to cry, to grieve, on the mistaken assumption that it isn't manly. Many older executives are in this group. Their wives have never worked because that was the norm at the time they were married. Also, the job loss may coincide with mid-life crisis. The men may feel that they didn't get where they wanted to go, they already have feelings of malaise, a vague dissatisfaction with themselves. Unemployment may occur just at the time of greatest expenditure, with one or more children in college. They aren't able to provide, so being unemployed functions as proof that they haven't "cut the mustard."

The married men whose wives work have a little more financial breathing room. They are going to get more realistic emotional support from their wives. But they have less freedom to relocate than the sole-support male.

Divorced males may already feel they have failed because of their divorce. The job loss is simply additional confirmation that they are failures, they don't measure up.

The single male is less predictable. He may be single by choice with a full complement of male and female friends. Or, he may be a loner, married to his job. Or any of a number of other possibilities. What's most important is the strength of his support groups.

Most male executives belong to the "old boy network." At least, they usually have a network of friends and business acquaintances in place who can be called upon for help and support. They also generally have well-defined careers developed over a longer period of time than many female executives. They may have worked for bigger, better firms. And, they probably started at higher employment levels than the older female executive who most frequently entered the job market in a lesser position.

Women do not have the "old boy network" tradition. When they do have networks in place, they are more likely to be social, not business networks, although this is changing. The divorced woman who was divorced while she still had children at home may have no network at all because she essentially worked three full-time jobs as mother, householder and wage earner. Her sole support group was her children. Now, even though they may be out on their own, the mother may still find she has not developed a replacement support group. She contacts her children for help. They react adversely—are frightened because their mother is frightened. Or, they may not be around to help. The divorced mother may also have entered the job market later and probably has fewer financial resources.

The married female executive, on the other hand, may find herself in a position where her out-of-work status is not taken seriously. In fact, she may not have the severe financial problems of the single and divorced woman executive. But she still has the same ego need to work as any other male or female executive and may find herself frustrated by a lack of empathy. Her networks are also generally social, not business.

Single females often are part of a well-developed network, either business or social. Or they may belong to both types of networks. They may not have as great financial needs as the divorced woman, but their job is usually their only source of financial support.

But most out-of-work women executives feel they have one emotional advantage over their male cohorts. They can cry because society allows it. They can grieve and get it out of their systems. Thus, their emotional rebirth may take less time than that of the male.

What's in This Book for You?
In the four parts following, you will be asked to become an active participant in taking charge of your future—at least the working part of your future. In part I, you'll develop a personal action plan. This includes setting up a job search regime, organizing your time and working efficiently at the job search, taking care of your appearance and health and putting your finances in order. You also will spend time evaluating yourself—who and what you are—and planning the contacts you should make to begin your job search. You'll also find some suggestions for coping with your number one problem—the emotional traumas associated with unemployment—so that you can, in the words of a recent off-Broadway show, "get your act together and take it on the road."

Part II is short, but important. It suggests some activities you should go through to set your employment goals. What kind of job should you search for? What you have been doing—or should you make a career change, perhaps even go into business for yourself? What kind of business should you approach to work in—small business or industry or Fortune 500? Will you insist on a job on the level you just left (or higher)—or are you willing to "settle," to accept a lesser job just to work? And you also should take a good look back at the job you just left. Were you really unfairly treated? If you were, should you take legal action?

Part III contains the "nuts and bolts" activities you will have to engage in before you are again among the working. You'll review the various types of resumes and how to write each (and which is most appropriate for each communication style or job type). You will also be reminded of the various ways to research jobs, seek out agencies and employment services and prospects for jobs. You will have a chance to update your letter-writing style so you don't present yourself as "old." And you'll get help on interviewing.

In Part IV, you'll take a look at the evaluation and decision process. When do you accept a job offer? Should you refuse it (or them) and hold out for more? And finally, after you accept an employment offer, what do you do to make sure you stay on this new job?

Part 1
Developing a Personal Action Plan

Coping with Emotions

The basis of the unhappiness and fears of the unemployed older executive *is* related to age. If you are to become an effective job seeker, you need first to understand *why* unemployment has such an adverse effect upon you—and to learn that it affects others in the same ways as well. Then, you have to understand and begin the adaptations that will allow you to function in as near a normal manner as is possible during that "abnormal" state of unemployment. By discussing the emotional problems of unemployment with others in the same boat and taking some action, you can again feel in charge of yourself and, to some extent, of your destiny. You can arrive on the other side increased in stature, not destroyed as a person.[1]

Emotional Stages of Unemployment

Older executives vary widely in their reactions to unemployment.

---

1. The information in this chapter is based on interviews with Scott Budge, a group counseling specialist at Pace University in New York City. Since 1979, Budge has worked regularly with a group of unemployed executives, managers and professionals in a one and a half hour per week "Rap Session." In these sessions, attendees express their feelings and attempt to come to grips with their emotional problems. The members of the group participated in a longitudinal study Budge conducted to establish the basis of their feelings of anger, fear and general inability to cope. Many of the insights Budge developed over this period of time are included. In addition to the interviews, he graciously shared a preliminary draft of an article on the same topic he coauthored with Ronald W. Janoff, director, Management Institute of New York University.

But regardless of differences in personality and in ability to cope, most go through three emotional stages during the period they are unemployed, according to Scott Budge, a group counseling specialist at Pace University. Those stages are: job loss, balance/ dismay and adaptation.

STAGE 1: *Job Loss*. During this stage, older executives are disoriented—they have suddenly lost their daily routine. They have to face telling their family and friends of the loss, and anticipate their shock and anger. Family reactions are relatively predictable, and executives dread these responses. In fact, many male executives go for weeks without telling their families they're unemployed. Friends, on the other hand, are almost always initially supportive; but too many of them seem to "fade away" as the period of unemployment lengthens.

Older executives' immediate reactions are generally of confusion, not depression. Some have a feeling of suspension in time—even elation. They may take a vacation or time off as means of avoiding facing what will be a severe loss. They emotionally flip-flop between concern over economic factors (how will they get along without their income, benefits, etc., how will they meet their expenses?) and anger over their job loss.

They begin their job search with exaggerated confidence. They're sure they'll have no trouble finding a new job. This confidence remains if they're successful, but soon evaporates if they have to spend eight months or more looking for a replacement position.

STAGE 2: *Balance/Dismay*. Most unemployed older executives make some kind of arrangements about their financial spending within two months—they reduce outgo, refinance, file for unemployment, etc. This reduces their immediate worries about money, although the worry remains just below the surface. And they achieve emotional distance from the job loss.

But the initial feeling of loss is replaced by a growing dismay that finding a job is not within their control and that the most frequent response to their job search efforts is silence. They become puzzled and may be immobilized. Pessimism takes over. They may reinterpret their preceding weeks' efforts as vain or unrealistic—or a waste of time. As one executive put it:

> I've absolutely wasted seven weeks of my life. My resumé is not good, every contact I've made has been unproductive. I didn't have seven weeks to waste. I feel like I'm just splattering. And I've always been focused.

Their self-esteem erodes from within. They become convinced that "something is wrong with me." They really feel that people can look at them and tell they are unemployed. They ask questions like: "Can anyone tell I'm out of work?" They don't sleep at night. They feel abnormal. They often become depressed.

This is the stage at which older executives seek help from professional counselors, buy self-help books (like this one), go to search firms, even seek psychoanalysis. Budge says they often address questions to counselors which are really requests to know how they are supposed to feel. "I don't sleep at night. Am I depressed?" or "Is it *normal* to feel this way?"

During this period, they struggle against their loss of self-confidence. A new routine which masks the pain of unemployment with the trappings of daily working life is usually the result. This is illustrated by the comment:

> You've gotta get away from the house, because that's death. I get up every morning, put on a shirt and tie. Then I get the hell out. I make myself do it. I have a routine and I stick to it. But what I really want to do is get back to work so the routine counts for something.

STAGE 3: *Adaptation*. The newly developed routine becomes the basis for the third stage, adaptation. The routines are a protective ritual against self-doubt and frustration. Unemployed older executives must struggle continually to assure themselves that things are OK, that everything will work out all right, even though they realize that their sense of personal worth is tied up with their worth to an organization—and that to be employed is to be employed for someone, not merely by someone.

As time goes on and they still have no employment, they learn to manage their days to protect their positive sense of self and to keep the realities of their situations invisible. They may increase their participation in community affairs, proceed with businesslike activity (appointments, calls) and keep to a time schedule. Their job hunt will probably be more continuous, better organized and sophisticated, even though rejection continues. Because this activity, which should be productive, is not, their notions of reward for activity are upset and they worry continuously over the causes of rejection.

During the adaptation stage, a support group of some sort becomes especially useful. A group provides urgently needed feedback from peers and gives them an opportunity to vent their "hidden" fears about skills displacement, age, general worthlessness and obsolescence.

Issues to Resolve During the Adaptive Phase of Unemployment

Whether unemployed older executives join a support group or not, they still have four major issues they must resolve during the adaptive phase. They are: identity maintenance, loss of office, persistence of guilt and ambivalence in relationships.

1. *Identity Maintenance.* By now, most unemployed executives refer to themselves in generic terms—I'm a planner, a manager of information systems, a sales manager, a marketing manager, a purchasing manager, a controller or financial officer. They avoid reference to their former companies and to their former specific job title. They describe their skills and accomplishments in a textbook (read that resumé) style. As they talk about themselves, they seem to be rehearsing for their interviews. By generalizing their skills, they also mask a worry that their specific job-related skills will melt away—that they'll be obsolete.

Even though still unemployed, they identify strongly with work roles, career direction, and with the drive and rewards that are provided by an organization. By being deprived of a job, they are deprived of the context in which managing can be formally performed and of the organizational goals to which their very genuine skills were attuned. So, they have a real need to retain this organizational identity even in the absence of an institution.

We've got to be marketable, in tune with the '80s. Management is looking for a quick payback or they go down the tubes. So we all try to show how cost-efficient we are, how profitable it will be for a company to hire us because of our skills and knowledge.

The income is the measure of somebody's assessment of our value to them. I don't think I can afford to—or stand to—work for less than 30 grand.

I've gotta do something. I want to stay in my field, I want to do something good, to work for a company. I want to be rewarded. Maybe I'm just geared to the work ethic. I always like to be busy, even if I just paint my house or start a vegetable garden. Even if I say, OK, you're going to do nothing. I still set a goal that that's what I'll do. I've got to know the direction I'm headed and know what my plan is. That's the worst thing about being unemployed—I don't really know where I'm going.

I've always been very goal-oriented—most of us have. We get to a certain place and discover most of our goals have been set for us by whatever business we were in. Now, we don't have those things driving us and we discover we don't have any personal goals. If we don't reset some goals, we're not going to get well. We don't even know what to be challenged by.

2. *Loss of Office.* The loss of an office critically undermines the struggle to maintain executive identity. The "office" confers and signals status and identity. It's the forum in which executives practice their craft. But something else happens with the loss of the office. Before, home and work were separated, with home being the privileged location where one relaxed, had leisure and privacy. Now, home is neither fish nor fowl—it is neither itself nor the office. It is no longer sanctuary. So unemployed executives find they have no place that's their own, no office and no home.

In addition, all the normal, routine accouterments of the office are no longer available. They don't have access to an answered telephone, to a typist, to a photocopy machine, even to simple supplies. They must take a great deal of time and personal initiative to accomplish even the simplest task.

3. *Persistence of Guilt.* Unemployed older executives must struggle with potentially immobilizing feelings of guilt. Regardless of cause, the job loss almost always converts into personal terms of guilt. And President Reagan's campaign quip that "when the other guy is out of work, it's a recession; when you're out of work, it's a depression" too often becomes a reality. As the experience of unemployment continues, depression shifts from its economic meaning to its psychological meaning and the individual is threatened with that as well.

The sense of guilt arises from several sources. For instance, most older executives have been "brainwashed," if you will, by the Protestant work ethic—you feel you don't have value if you're not being productive. It's an insidious thing, with even routine things like a coffee break losing their value because you no longer have work to take a break from! The popular press and even friends and family give a negative moral value to being unemployed. Unemployment is equated with morally unjustified idleness, with laziness.

> I feel very negative about myself. My family expected more of me. I disappointed them. I'm the guilty one. But being unemployed proves Daddy was right—I am nothing. I'm scared to death to apply for a new job. I can't face new judgments.

> Every time I get turned down, I beat myself to death. I go through a whole series of why did I's and I should have's. If I'd just handled something differently, I would have gotten the job.

Unemployed older executives develop a personal focus of self-blame which disables. They experience unemployment as a sign that they're failures. They discount any previous accomplishments. They may have an unreasonable sense of "destiny" which says that fate caused their unemployment because they were inadequate. They may develop a circular pattern of blame. "I am no good because no one will hire me. But that's the way things are. The economy is bad, so the company had to let people go. But why me? I may really be no good. After all, no one has hired me . . ." They have a nagging sense of worthlessness which dogs their steps.

Each interview, then, becomes a personal test on a deep level. They worry whether the interviewer "saw" their lack of value. And this anxiety may cause them to present themselves in an artificial and constrained manner, undermining the interview.

But older executives must fight their feelings of personal worthlessness and daily affirm the value of work and of working by actively seeking employment. The actual act of looking for work may help harness the feelings. So, the ritualization of an imitation of working—dressing, commuting, maintaining a visible aspect of a working routine—becomes extremely important. It represents control over the situation, a sort of magical force working for the individual to counteract the feelings of being lost and worthless.

4. *Ambivalence in Relationships*. The unemployed older executive's role is strained by the conditions of unemployment. Relationships with family and friends become ambivalent. Even if the individual joins a group whose stated purpose is to help the person get work, relationships tend to be awkward and a little constrained simply because unemployment may be "contagious." As John F. says: "Friends ask how you are doing, but they're petrified they may also lose their jobs."

This ambivalence further aggravates self-doubt and causes people to have an almost perpetual preoccupation with the impression they are making on others. They are particularly concerned with the impressions they're making on interviewers.

> I'm feeling negative about myself, so I think I'm being abrasive. I'm sending out negative signals and getting negative feedback. I haven't had such negative feedback in years. I've even had out-and-out run-ins with people and I've been decimated. My God, if that's the way I'm coming across, how can I possibly go out and get a job?"

They are also profoundly lonely. Even though many older executives may be out of a job, they are individually out of work, not like labor groups, which may all be out of work temporarily because of a layoff or something like that. When older executives do get jobs, they will get them alone—by themselves.

Budge describes unemployment as a group phenomenon by using

this analogy: Unemployment is like a group of commuters waiting for a bus. Each line of people (job applicants) is waiting for a bus (job) to come in, without knowledge of the bus driver's (employer's) exact position or even whether the bus (company) has broken down (layoffs, belt-tightening, hiring freezes). The bus driver is just doing a job (hiring) and doesn't know the passengers (applicants), nor in any way grasps their individual concerns. When a bus does finally arrive, if it isn't one's own, the destinations of its passengers are irrelevant.

Some Guidelines to
Handling the Emotions of Unemployment

Since managerial identity is threatened by unemployment, the development of ritual activities, of a job search routine, buffers the psychological ill effects. Budge recommends as particularly helpful the following:

- Accept that unemployment is a contingency in your career. Deal promptly with family and income problems to avoid destabilization. Maintain professional contacts and professional visibility as an aspect of working life that you can mobilize during unemployment. Continue your leisure-time activities, a hobby, small business or community activity and investigate them to see if they are exploitable reserve resources.
- Locate and associate with others who are also unemployed. Such relationships are inherently unstable, but they can be incorporated into a ritual of businesslike activity which is focused on getting a new job. It also helps substitute for the informal work relations and keeps alive the feelings of a peer group apart from family and friends. Such a group helps individuals discharge their constant feelings of worthlessness. The group gives consolation to the hurts and indignities of rejection, and provides a place to allow yourself to display your unemployed status without damage.
- Assess and reassess your status as a means of reaffirming the values of the business system without accepting any personal guilt. Decide for yourself which of the values you accept and

which no longer are important to you.

□ If you seek professional help, seek it wisely. Most of the problems of unemployment result from the condition itself. Many therapists and counselors lack a clear understanding of the determinants of these problems and may unwittingly enlarge an individual's feelings of self-blame. Many professionals have therapy models which are not based on work, and they are themselves peripheral to organizational life. Few have had training in problems related to worklife. They may apply clinical models, mistaking the mechanical depression of unemployment for physiological depression. As a result, they misdiagnose and give inappropriate treatment. (Frequently, depression clears up immediately when older executives are reemployed. If the depression were physiologically caused, this would not be true.)

Budge also emphasized the real need older unemployed executives have for emotional support of some kind. You need an opportunity to ventilate your feelings without becoming maudlin and without a judgment being made against you. Some ways to get this emotional support:

1. *Join an existing support group for unemployed older executives guided by a competent professional.* This has several advantages. First, the others in the group are your peers because of the selection process. Second, the composition of the group is fluid, varying from meeting to meeting with the entrance of new members and the departure of old members to jobs. Thus, it is easy for someone to fill a niche in the group. Third, the very fact that you are going to the group on a transitory basis may enable you to come to grips more readily with some deep feelings and real problems. Have you ever met someone you've never seen before and don't expect ever to see again with whom you developed instant rapport? During the course of your conversation, did you discuss inner secrets and feelings you'd never before bared to anyone? These groups operate somewhat on the same basis. You know you'll be understood—and you know what you say will not be held against you at a later date or under other circumstances.

2. *Your family.* If you have a family, they may be a good alternative to a support group. However, whether this is a valid option for you or not is situational. Do you already have open lines of communication with your spouse and/or children? If so, you are in a position to discuss your current feelings. In fact, the occasion of unemployment can act to draw families back together and to reopen formerly closed avenues of communication. This does require a great deal of effort on your part and you may feel that in your situation, it wouldn't work.

Brothers, sisters and cousins (who are, after all, built-in peers), may make a better support group than those with whom you reside. You have a common experience base, and they may have been unemployed at some time or other. So, if you have family members around, at least try to draw upon these lines of support.

3. *Friends.* You may encounter problems in using friends as a basis of support. But you still should try. Use care in approaching them. Don't make them feel threatened about their own status. Also, keep in mind that some people may be embarrassed if you attempt to use them as a "crying towel." Most, however, are willing to listen and will help if you can give them some reasonable way they can. Perhaps those friends best able to give you support and good advice are those who have, at some time in the past, grappled with unemployment themselves. Review your friends for this kind of experience. Then perhaps invite several who fit this criterion over for an hour or two or phone them to talk.

Should any of your friends or acquaintances happen to be currently unemployed, you have a real opportunity to develop a mutual self-help organization with a broader purpose than just that of your own personal needs.

4. *Other existing sources of support.* If none of the preceding is available, check in your area to see what is. Call the business librarian at your local library. Contact one of the business editors or the librarian at your local newspaper. Approach your priest, rabbi or minister. Go by the Chamber of Commerce, the YMCA, YWCA, YMHA, YWHA. Check with local college counseling services, the personnel department of your former employer (if you parted under amicable conditions). Other possible contacts are the

local mental health agencies. And, at least discuss the question of this kind of support with a counselor at the unemployment office.

Keep in mind, though, that the kind of emotional support you are looking for is likely to be different from that needed to further your job search.

For those few of you whose drinking habits may have contributed toward your current unemployed status, don't overlook the very real help and support of groups such as Alcoholics Anonymous. Numerous AA members have already struggled with the twin problems of alcoholism and unemployment. Locate meetings whose attendees will most likely come from the executive, professional or managerial ranks.

For some of you, prayer may be a means of getting support. In the strictly secular setting of unemployment, people tend to forget that other avenues of help exist. If you have a religious background and some experience with prayer, try it. It can't hurt—and it could be healing.

5. *Set up your own mutual support group.* If none of the above will work, then locate other unemployed older executives and set up your own group. Run an ad in a local paper or put up a notice on the community bulletin board. You can probably arrange to have a preliminary meeting in donated space—a church, a school or someone's office after hours. (In many communities, banks and savings and loans have meeting rooms which they'll make available free of charge to worthy community groups.)

To get such a group off the ground, you'll have to use your organizational, managerial and problem-solving skills. But you'll end up helping both yourself and others. And, you'll get the sort of support and lift to your self-esteem which you need.

This last alternative requires more commitment than the others if it is to be made to work. You will need to recruit someone to serve as a facilitator—perhaps a minister with counseling training, a high school counselor with special skills for working in group situations, or someone who regularly facilitates other types of group therapy. The group should be organized so that it can be ongoing after you get your own long-awaited job. Otherwise, it could be a disservice both to you and to the very people you want to recruit as members.

When you were employed, you disciplined your activities and structured your time. The external requirements of the job forced you to get up at 6:30 every morning, shower and shave or put on makeup in 10 minutes, eat breakfast, then commute to work. The rest of your day was similarly organized, culminating with a regular evening regime and bedtime at a reasonable hour. You probably always considered yourself very disciplined and perhaps looked down a little on others who were not.

Now, more than ever, make this lifetime of good habits work for you. Avoid the temptation to take some time off for good behavior. Don't go off on a vacation (unless it has been planned for months and you'd lose the cost of the tickets) or take the first few weeks off to "take care of some of the things around the house that have needed doing for years."

Once you let down, you'll find it more difficult to gear up for a concerted job search. But you don't feel like looking for a job, you say? You want time to lick your wounds and get yourself in shape? Some other time, perhaps, but not now.

Consider first the personal aspects of your job search. How are you going to keep your spirits up, use your time effectively, present your best side to potential employers? In other words, how are you going to get your act together?

Set Up a Job Search Regime

Think of a job search as a particularly tough business problem-solving activity, which includes:

1. Identifying and defining the problem.
2. Developing alternative solutions to the problem.
3. Evaluating solutions.
4. Making a decision.
5. Implementing the solution.

A Job Search as Problem Solving

In a job search, each one of these phases has a corresponding function particular to looking for a job. *Identifying and defining the problem* is the same as in standard problem solving. The second phase, *developing alternative solutions to the problem*, is more correctly named *conducting your job campaign*. Instead of calling the third phase evaluating solutions, you will be *evaluating the job opportunities and offers*. In phase four, you will still be *making a decision*, and in phase five, you will be implementing your decision as you *begin working* at a new job.

Identifying and Defining the Problem. In these activities, you are trying to find out about yourself, your strengths and weaknesses as well as the business environment in which you will be doing your job search. Begin the same as you would when you're solving a business problem. Determine first what the facts are. Ask yourself:

What have you done?

What are your strengths and weaknesses? Specific technical, business and interpersonal skills? What deficits in these areas have caused you difficulties in the past? (See Chapters 4 and 5, pp. 43 to 86.)

Where might you locate a job? This ranges all the way from researching possible job sources in directories to determining what recruiters or employment agencies to contact, developing lists of firms to approach, to taking advantage of your friends and associates in making potential employment contacts. (Chapters 3 and 6 offer help with this, pp. 33-42 and 89-103.)

At the same time, you determine your employment objectives.

You want to decide what kind of job you want, the salary you require, and whether you want to change job types or consider trying a second career. (Chapter 5.)

Then analyze your situation. Take into account the employment opportunities in your area, any deficits which you have to overcome, your current financial situation, and outside factors such as family, health, training, relocation, children's education, etc.

You can consider that you've properly defined the problem when you've decided what you think will be the most useful approaches to try in your job search and you've developed a reasonable schedule to follow. As a final step, you should also prepare an interim resumé to use immediately. (See Chapter 7, page 105.)

Conducting Your Job Campaign. During this phase, you'll do everything possible to look for job opportunities, make contacts and get interviews. You'll do some or all of the following activities and more:

- Develop a good resumé (or series of resumés). (Chapter 7.)
- Contact friends and acquaintances for information and help. (Networking—see Chapter 3, pp. 37-40.)
- Contact any and all groups and agencies which might help you with your search. (Chapter 3, pp. 40-42 and Chapter 6, pp. 91-92.)
- Answer advertisements, write letters, telephone for appointments, etc. (Chapter 6, pp. 95-103, and all of Chapter 8.)
- Apply directly to companies for which you'd like to work.
- Join organizations for job search help and support.

Your job campaign should also include definite action toward resolving the personal deficits you've identified. If you need additional training, find where you can get it and begin. Pay attention to your physical appearance and health. Act to rid yourself of personal hang-ups and personal problems unrelated to your job search which lessen your job hunting effectiveness. Optional: Join a support group, seek personal help through counseling.

Learning successful interviewing skills—how to recognize the interviewer's communication style; how to answer, ask and counter questions; how to present yourself most favorably and how to keep the job offer alive are invaluable in conducting a successful job campaign. (Chapters 4, 9 and 10 cover these topics in detail.)

Evaluate the Job Opportunities and Offers. This part is crucial. Far too frequently, unemployed people, especially older executives who have been out of work for an inordinately long time, will grasp at straws, accepting jobs which are unsuitable and which they will not keep for long. You must look for a match between yourself and your potential employer or job opportunity. You don't have the time a younger person has to make a mistake on your job selection. Otherwise, you may again be among the unemployed, with greater damage to your self-esteem than you had the first time around.

Consider first whether you should accept the position or opportunity:

- Do you fit the job characteristics?
- Would it be challenging? Would you enjoy it? Find it fun?
- What about your potential employer (company)? Do your values match those of the company and your prospective boss(es)?
- What about the salary? Benefits? The responsibilities you'd have? Freedom of action? Opportunities?
- What are the shortcomings of the situation? Do they outweigh the positive aspects or vice versa?

If you feel that job is desirable, what about negotiating with the company to change some of the undesirable elements? Will you have an opportunity to negotiate about salary, relocation allowances, benefits, perquisites, or the scope of the position? (See Chapter 11.)

Making a Decision. Should you be among the extremely fortunate and have more than one job opportunity or offer (or even if you have only one offer), you still have to make your decision. Will you accept the position? (Or which of several positions you've been offered will you accept?) Or, must you continue looking for something more suitable? Don't make a mistake and accept the position if the offers are not for something you should do.

Beginning Work. And, finally, comes another difficult task—implementing your decision and beginning work. Now that you've accepted a position, what can you do to ensure that you are successful on the new job, that the match between you and your new employer works? (Some hints are included in Chapter 11.)

Time Management—Working Efficiently

Job hunting is time consuming and exhausting. You must use your time as effectively as possible. You're used to managing time on your job. But when you're unemployed, everything else is out of whack, and it's awfully easy to quit managing your time, too. This section on time management isn't meant to be insulting—it's meant as a reminder to continue managing your time wisely.

One of the most efficient time management tools is the list. Begin by writing down as many job hunting activities as you can think of, basing them on the suggestions shown earlier in this chapter in the section on *identifying and defining the problem.* Then prioritize the activities, using an A, B, C system. (A for the most immediately critical activities, B for those which are important but can wait a while, C for those which might be useful to do but can be done later, provided doing the A and B items doesn't get you a job.) Then, for those rating an A priority, number, in order of importance and/or immediate need.

Let's say your list looks like this:

□ Read job hunting books.
□ Talk to other unemployed or recently unemployed executives or professionals to find out what worked for them.
□ Write a preliminary resumé.
□ Make a list of your accomplishments on the job. What you did that set you apart from someone else with the same kind of job.
□ Write job descriptions for each position you held.
□ List responsibilities for each position held.

- ◻ Review your strengths in technical, business and interpersonal skills. Write them down.
- ◻ Evaluate your technical, business and interpersonal weaknesses. Decide if you have any areas where you should take corrective action.
- ◻ Determine and write your job objective or objectives, if you are qualified or interested in more than one kind of position.
- ◻ Write a thumbnail description highlighting your business abilities.
- ◻ Prepare drafts of your final resumé or resumés. You may need several different kinds and may go through several drafts before you come up with something you can use.
- ◻ Get personal stationery printed.
- ◻ Locate a good typist, if you don't type yourself or have access to a personal computer/word processor.
- ◻ Review personal wardrobe for job hunting suitability.
- ◻ Find a place to work outside your house—the office of a friend, the public library, etc.
- ◻ Arrange to have your telephone answered—answering service or machine, someone's office.
- ◻ Apply for unemployment compensation.
- ◻ Review your financial obligations and finances.
- ◻ Prepare a budget for six months or longer.
- ◻ Get your resumé drafts reviewed by knowledgeable people in your field, or by people whose opinion you value.
- ◻ Prepare answers to possible interview questions.
- ◻ Go through at least one and preferably more mock interviews with friends, acquaintances or other job seekers.
- ◻ Discuss your situation fully and honestly with your family.
- ◻ Seek help from a counselor.
- ◻ Contact all of your references, in person preferably, or by telephone.

Obviously, this list is incomplete. But you could use it as a starter, supplementing it with items of your own. You can see that all of these can't be done in one day, one week, or even one month. After all, you aren't superman or superwoman! So, concentrate initially on those items that you will need immediately and tag them as having an A priority. One possible A list, shown in prioritized order: (Your own list will be different.)

Priority	Activity
A1.	Write a preliminary resumé.
A2.	Apply for unemployment compensation.
A3.	Review your financial obligations and finances.
A4.	Discuss your situation fully and honestly with your family.
A5.	Get personal stationery printed.
A6.	Locate a typist.

Then, at the start of every day, list the activities you should work on for that day, reprioritizing according to the A, B, C system. Be sure to include personal-care activities like getting a haircut, shining your shoes, taking clothing to the cleaners, going to the beauty shop, etc.

As you complete each essential preliminary activity, check it off on your personal checklist. This will keep you on target and give you a sense of accomplishment. Then, continue to make lists and check off activities as you enter the later phases of your job search problem solving.

Keep in mind another point about time management. The experts say, "Do it now." In looking for work, it's entirely too easy for you to procrastinate and spend hours "fiddling around" or otherwise wasting time. Instead, consider your job search to be full-time employment—perhaps the most important job of your life, since it will determine your continued success. Let's face it. At this age, there's a terrible temptation just to give up and let everything go. Fight it.

Get up in the morning at your regular time. Eat a good breakfast. Get dressed in your business togs. *Get going.* Leave the house with your briefcase and your list for the day. Then, put in at least a six-hour work day toward completing your A priorities—those activities you identified as most important *today* toward your job search. By doing this, you are making an active commitment toward finding a job.

Keep accurate and complete records. They'll help you stay on track, paying attention to proper time utilization. And you need them to evaluate your progress.

Your Appearance and Health

After your years in the executive ranks, reminding you that appearance is a critical hiring element may seem presumptuous. This section is simply a reminder of the importance that appearance plays, and suggests that you take a good look at yourself as others see you. If your appearance doesn't measure up to some interviewer's preconceptions, you've provided an automatic "deselector," with nothing else that occurs in the interview really counting. But paying special attention to your appearance each day has another, perhaps more important and personal value. That is, "the better you know you look, the better you'll feel about yourself." It's a way of whistling in the dark, of keeping your spirits up.

Listen to S. Eric Wachtel, president, Wachtel Associates, a firm specializing in executive recruitment and organizational planning and development:

> Far too many older executives reinforce the stereotypes which produce hiring prejudices. They don't pay attention to their personal appearance and general presentation. I continue to be astonished at the number who come into this office needing a haircut and wearing messy shirts with frayed collars and cuffs. Their suits are rumpled and either lack taste or are out of style. Their entire appearance—lack of general grooming, poor posture, low energy level—screams, "This person is a poor risk. Don't consider hiring him or her." They appear defeated, and reinforce this impression when they speak. Their voices are weak and shaky; they are either obsequious or overly engaging—too up. They completely fail to sell themselves, to present a positive image.[1]

Clothing. Begin by taking a really good look at your wardrobe. Check each garment for pulls, loose buttons, frayed cuffs, etc. Then put on the suits that pass muster and stand in front of a full-length

---

1. S. Eric Wachtel just published a book called *How to Hold on to Your Job.* If you'd read it soon enough, you wouldn't have to read this one!

mirror. Do the suits fit smoothly, without wrinkles or unusual bulges?

Consider: How long has it been since you bought a good new suit? If your answer is a year or more ago, this is one place you can't economize. Go to a first-class shop and buy a new suit, complete with new shirt (or blouse), shoes, and other appropriate accessories. Buy in tasteful, muted, somewhat conservative colors (blues, grays) in natural fibers (wool, silk, cotton). If the store has a wardrobe coordinator, ask for his/her help and accept the recommendations he or she makes. Then, have the suit tailored to fit. Don't cut corners here.

Hair. Next, look at your hair. Are you waiting too long between haircuts? Go to a barber or hairdresser and get a good style cut. Consider carefully your present hairstyle. Can it be a deselector? Anything which interviewers look on unfavorably or which hits on any of their preconceptions or prejudices should be avoided. Some possible examples: Males still wearing crewcuts may be viewed as too military, reactionary or rigid, or simply as failing to keep current. (If you have this style, you probably view it as the easy way to take care of your hair. All you do is scrub and go! But look at it carefully from the interviewer's viewpoint and make your decision to keep or grow accordingly.) Women who wear their hair long and "down" may give the impression that they are reaching backward frantically for youth. (If you like wearing your hair long, then at least put it up into a businesslike chignon or in a clasp at the nape of your neck. But above all, avoid the sophisticated, but unbusinesslike "updo.") Better yet, consider cutting your hair and wearing it in a short, softly waved, but unteased style.

Men: If you've been going to the corner barbershop for years just because it's handy—then find out who cuts the hair of the person you know with the best-looking hairstyle—then go to that stylist to get your own cut.

Women: Continue your regular visits to your hairdresser. Don't wait to get a permanent or begin doing your own hair as a money-saving measure. You need to look your very best. If you haven't been going to a hairdresser regularly, invest in hair care to improve your overall image.

Job counselors, employment agency personnel and executive recruiters disagree on whether to color hair or not. It may be a matter of personal preference. But many of the job hunters feel that anything which might give them an appearance edge in locating a job should be considered. If you decide in favor of coloring, be careful. If you had black or dark brown hair, don't have your hair dyed back to its original dark color. It always looks artificial and gives a harsh, unflattering edge you don't need. Instead, go for a lighter, softer brown than your natural color. Since you will already be coloring, you can at least go for the most flattering effect. The distinction between male and female hairdressing establishments has blurred, so the place to have your hair dyed would be at a beauty shop with a colorist. Above all, don't attempt to color your hair yourself—the results will most likely not be the effect you desire. And if you decide to color, you must pay special attention to the roots and get regular two- to three-week touch-ups.

A few years ago, the preceding would have been out of place for male managers, although acceptable for women. However, today's executives are more adaptable—and it is a way to present a slightly more youthful appearance.

Another hair question which must be dealt with is what to do if your hairline is decidedly receding (or, let's face it, if you're bald). Again, the general impression is better if you just accept the bald spot instead of doing a fancy trick—combing eight-inch side hair over the gleaming top in the vain hope that the shine won't show. It *always* shows, and this hairstyle is rarely flattering. Sometimes the part is so low that almost no short hair is left above the sideburns! The question of wearing a toupee or wig is in the same area of taste. If you have a very good hand-tied toupee or wig of real hair which fits exceptionally well—and is the same color as your sideburns and lower back hair, then wear it. But take a critical and honest look at the image you present in the mirror. Is it obvious that you are wearing a "rug"? It's your decision if you want to continue with your hair that way, or go to the expense of getting a really good hairpiece—which costs several hundred dollars.

General grooming. A couple of other appearance notes. Spend more time on regular grooming. Take extra care during your bath or shower. Keep your nails trimmed and buffed, or have a regular manicure. Keep your shoes polished and have new heel lifts put on as soon as the heels even begin to wear. Have your suits cleaned and pressed more frequently. And take the necessary time to exercise and keep yourself trim. It's awfully easy just to give in to gravity and let everything sag!

Posture. Posture projects self-image. Even if you don't feel like it, put on your best posture whenever you leave your house. Gather your body together, lift your chest, relax your shoulders, tuck under your derrière and straighten your spine. See, you already look better! Finish the good impression by keeping your head up, ready to look the world in the eye. And stride when you walk—use energy in this and your other body movements—but the energy of a strong body, not nerves.

So what if that isn't the way you feel—fake it. Act. You are doing a very important selling job—selling yourself into a job. And that has to begin by selling yourself on yourself. After you force yourself to present a lively appearance, you will find that the reality will soon come to approximate the presentation, and you'll feel better for it. Practice walking, sitting and standing with energy. Then check the way you look doing it in a full-length mirror. (That full-length mirror has to function as your toughest critic.) As you walk down the street, continue to observe yourself in store windows as you pass by. Make adjustments constantly to keep up your posture and your positive appearance.

Health and physical well-being. After you have your external appearance under control, consider your internal being. Get a physical to check on your health status. Find out if there is a physical cause for your general malaise and lack of energy. Check on your nutritional status—when you're "down," it's too easy to skimp on your meals and fail to get adequate amounts of vitamins, minerals and other nutrients. It is another of those vicious-cycle things—you don't feel well, so you don't eat well. You don't eat well, so you don't feel well. And, of course, check on the condition of your heart and vascular system.

If you have been troubled by impotence or a total disinterest in sex, don't accept for one minute that this is totally due to your age or is completely tied in to your unemployed state (although that can definitely bear on the problem). Bring up the topic and discuss it fully and frankly with your doctor.

If you are not having any of these problems, you should still get a physical. Just knowing that your general health is all right, or that you are doing something about it, will be of value and will help increase your self-esteem.

Put Your Finances in Order

Your income for the immediately foreseeable future has been drastically reduced. Even if your last employer gave you a healthy severance package, you're not prescient. You don't know how long you will be unemployed. For example: in the recent recession of 1981-83, the length of unemployment for managers averaged somewhere between eight months and one year. Of course, some managers found immediate reemployment. But for each manager in that happy circumstance, a corresponding manager had already been searching one year to eighteen months, depending to some extent upon the health of the business or industry in which he or she was searching for work.

So taking prudent financial steps immediately is essential, even if you'd rather just continue the way you are. Don't be an ostrich—be realistic, instead, as you review your situation.

1. *Apply for unemployment compensation immediately.* Far too many older managers and professionals fail to apply soon enough for this income source out of a misplaced sense of pride. Then when they finally do apply, they discover they cannot recover the funds which would have been available to them between the end of their employment and the time they applied. If you didn't go because you had accrued vacation time, the unemployment divisions of the various states automatically take this into account in calculating when they will begin paying benefits. There is always a period of delay between filing and the first check. So run, not walk, to get your application in so you don't lost any of the funds to which you are legitimately entitled.

2. *Go over your current budget.* If you don't have one, check your actual expenditures for the last six months to determine your current spending levels.

- List essential expenditures—food, utilities, mortgage, health insurance, tuition payments. (If any of your children are still in school, you will want to avoid taking them out of college if you can, since this will probably be upsetting to you. However, you might insist he or she get a job to help with his or her expenses.)
- List other expenditures for which you are obligated—car payments, loans, etc.
- List expenditures you think you'll have to make during your job campaign. Don't cheat yourself and the success of your campaign by trying to cut corners on these. You must have resumés printed, you should have personalized stationery and you'll need operating expenses—car, bus or train fare, lunch money, etc. Also include personal-care items such as needed new apparel and more frequent haircuts and/or beauty shop appointments.
- List items which are discretionary and can be cut. Cable TV, liquor, entertainment and country club dues fall in this category.

3. *Identify and list available income and other funds* you will have for at least the next six months. Include unemployment compensation.

4. *Take the necessary action to reinvest your pension funds if you aren't vested in your former employer's pension system.* You have only 60 days to rollover these funds into an IRA account. Don't miss the deadline. If you do, you won't be able to shelter the funds and you'll have to handle the moneys as regular income on your tax return. One other point: If you absolutely run out of funds, your pension or your IRAs could be used as collateral on a loan. And they're always there as a backup if your financial situation becomes desperate. Cashing in IRAs or pension funds should be your absolute last resort, especially since there are sizable penalties for early withdrawal of funds from these accounts.

5. *List other possible sources of funding*—the borrowing value of your life insurance, what you might get from refinancing your home, your stocks and bonds, IRAs, etc. You hope you won't have to tap these sources, but be realistic. What resources do you have?

6. *Work out a revised six-month budget.* If funds are going to be tight, contact your creditors and try to defer or rearrange payments on some of your major bills. Most creditors would prefer to know this in advance so they don't continue to push too hard. Notifying them also shows your "good faith intentions." You can avoid potential credit problems by taking this step early and working out a minimum payment schedule until you are again employed. Utility companies will often work with you, as they do with others, to equalize payments during this time.

7. *Set up an accounting procedure to keep track of your job search expenditures.* Many of these will be tax deductible.

8. *Discuss your projected budget fully with other family members.*

□ Men: If your wife hasn't been working, perhaps she will be willing to help tide the family over during this time by finding short-term work. If she is already employed, she may be able to take over the health insurance obligations for the family through her employer's health benefit package, for example.
□ Women: Discuss your revised budget and curtailed spending needs with your husband. Work out future spending together, since he will also have to work on a limited spending plan.
□ Families with children: Consider what contribution children remaining at home can make to the budget. At your age, they should be old enough to understand what is going on. Be sure to let them know what the problems will be, without scaring them unduly. They will be more helpful and less demanding if they know reality rather than having to conjecture the situation themselves. They also need to know you aren't "crying wolf." They may be able to take care of some of their own needs through part-time jobs or entrepreneurial pursuits such as yard

work, window washing, etc. Older children who are working, but still living at home, should be required to contribute at least enough for their own support.

□ Single: If you have no family responsibilities, then sit down and have a talk with a friend or relative—or with yourself—about your financial situation.

Whatever you do, come out of your deliberations with a workable financial plan that takes your situation fully into account. By doing so, you'll have your credit rating and the major portion of your resources intact at the end of this period of unemployment. And you'll accomplish something else as well. Financial problems exacerbate the bad feelings you already have because you're unemployed. Developing a financial plan and taking action is positive and productive and will give you a needed boost.

Recreation and Leisure-Time Activities

The stress of daily living is much harder on the unemployed than on someone who works 40 hours a week, according to Susan Barstis, a clinical psychologist with the Kaiser Permanente medical program in Los Angeles.[1] She suggests that the out-of-work need vacations more than people who are employed. But because most unemployed shouldn't spend the money for a typical vacation, she suggests less costly alternatives such as gardening, painting or carpentering—for a few hours each day. She says it will help relieve the trauma of job loss and perhaps can even ward off depression.

Older executives often are active in community affairs. There's a terrible temptation to withdraw from these activities when you're unemployed to avoid embarrassment. Don't yield to this desire. Continue to participate exactly as you did before. You'll get reinforcement of your continued worth—the organizations need you just as much now as they did before. And you'll have natural opportunities to meet other executives and may even get valuable leads on possible employment. Besides, when your unemployed period is over, you'll want to continue these desirable activities. If

---

1. Reported in *Psychology Today*, Vol. 17, No. 4, April 1983, p. 18.

you drop them now, you'll find them difficult to resume later. The only caution: don't let organizations and volunteer activities take over your life. You can't afford to spend your time on these to the detriment of your personal job search.

Finally, continue with your personal hobbies and with normal social activities. But keep this in perspective, too. You won't want to indulge in expensive entertaining or take up new and costly hobbies. But accept social outings, even if you really don't want to, and spend some time on those hobbies (the inexpensive ones) which give you the most pleasure.

Part 2
Taking Stock

When you're problem solving during your job search, you're really not working with a linear process. You'll move back and forth through different kinds of activities as your job search progresses and your situation changes. So, as soon as you complete a preliminary resumé, begin work on the activities suggested in *Conducting Your Job Campaign* (p. 17). Carry on those activities and those in this chapter at the same time. That way, you'll move your campaign along faster and make the most efficient use of your time. Both make contributions to more than one phase of the job search. And, some of them will serve you in good stead later when you're again among the working.

Early in your search, you're likely to have a tremendous urge to stay in your house or apartment and lick your wounds. You need to get yourself ready as quickly as you can to get out and make the necessary contacts to get things moving. However, you may make a grave error if you begin contacting people and companies before you really know exactly where you should be heading.

Find Out Who and What You Are

At this time in your life, your goals and your life in general have undergone major changes. Before you rush into a new job based on your old goals and life style, you need to evaluate carefully where you are right now—and where you want to go. The chances are you should change your life goals. You probably no longer really want the job which was your ultimate goal 10 to 20 years ago. Or, you may have already reached your initial goal and it's time for you to reset your goals instead of drifting aimlessly through this period. Take the time and effort to study yourself now. You may be surprised to find out how different your current needs and wants are from those you had in your twenties, thirties and even early forties.

Don't rush into a new job which is unsatisfactory for you. After a short time, you may quit, be terminated, or remain in an unhappy and possibly dead-end situation. In the 1980 edition of the *Directory of Outplacement Firms*, William J. Morin, president, director and CEO, Drake Beam Morin, Inc., stated this quite succinctly:

> Many individuals who are terminated after five, 10, 15 years with a company have a tendency to go out, find a job, and get themselves in trouble very quickly in their next position. They bounce from that job into the next job, and they experience this bouncing for a number of years. This is usually because they did not take time to ascertain what went wrong in the position from which they were first fired and to determine honestly the proper work environment in which they would be successful.

There are at least two ways of determining what you want to do with the rest of your life. You may contact an industrial psychologist or counseling firm—or you can study this on your own. Most job search specialists suggest that the most useful study is the one you undertake by yourself. But many people can't successfully complete this alone, either because they procrastinate or because they don't know where to start.

If you've already tried on your own and have decided to go for help, your first step is to locate a good, competent psychologist or counselor who isn't going to charge you an arm and a leg. Most universities have psychologists on their staffs who do this kind of counseling on a full- or part-time basis. You can also check with the American Personnel and Guidance Association for qualified practitioners in your area. In their *Directory of Approved Counseling Agencies*, they list those agencies in the various states which maintain high professional standards. Do take the time to check since this is an area with a high quackery content. Especially in these times of relatively high unemployment, someone is always around to take advantage of those who are experiencing adversity.

What should you expect from counseling? First, you should undergo a battery of psychological and skill evaluations. Then through a series of relatively structured interviews, you will review the results of your tests—your strengths, weaknesses, areas of interest, etc. Only then will you be ready to discuss and evaluate your job goals and objectives. This process should help you find out:

▢ If you are suited to the work you've been doing.
▢ What shortfalls or deficits you have that you can do something about.
▢ What your strengths are.
▢ What your interests are.
▢ What you should be doing.

If you decide to do this study on your own instead, you might begin with some clean sheets of paper. Head one sheet *Skills*, another *Strengths*, a third *Weaknesses*, a fourth *What I Want Out of a Job*, a fifth *Life style*, a sixth *Accomplishments* (subdivide this one into past, current and what I hope to do in the future), a seventh *Goals and Objectives* (subdivide this one into past, current and projected), and an eighth *Problems I Had on Earlier Jobs*. Keep a couple of other sheets handy for additional headings and for notes. Then answer the following questions on the appropriate sheet:

1. Is your existing career obsolete? Must you change careers because jobs are no longer available in your existing one?

2. What skills do you have? What do you do well? What do you enjoy?

3. What are your weaknesses? Have these caused you difficulty on the job? Which ones can be corrected—or should be corrected? Will this be costly in terms of time, effort or money?

4. What problems did you encounter in earlier jobs? If you were fired or terminated, what are the reasons? Be honest here. If it wasn't due to weakness on your part, say so. How can you avoid

these problems in the future?

5. What time spans are built into present decisions? For example: How long would additional training take? How much longer are your kids going to be in college? What risks are built into those decisions?

6. What goals, values, priorities do you already have?

7. What do you want to accomplish before you die? What do you perceive your life's mission to be? What have you already accomplished? Include both business and personal accomplishments.

8. What do you want out of a job? Do you like line or staff work, large or small companies? Do you prefer to be a specialist or would you rather have broad responsibilities? What kind of people do you like to work for and with? Can you be satisfied with a restricted job or do you require continual challenge? What about travel? Overtime or long hours on the job? What about long-term prospects for advancement? Do you prefer to "do" or to manage those who do?

9. Where do you want to work? In a major city, in a suburban area or in the country? What region of the country—Northeast, Southeast, Midwest, Southwest, Mountain States, Northwest, West Coast? Or do you prefer to work internationally? If so, where? Will you be willing to relocate or do you want to stay where you are?

10. What is your life style? Are you willing to make changes in it? Or are you happy with your current life style and unwilling to change if you don't have to?

After you have answered these questions (and others that you think of), analyze your answers carefully. The last step in completing your analysis is to develop your new goals and objectives. You may also want to write a narrative or summary statement which capsulizes who and what you are and where you want to go. You will find a partner useful in this endeavor. Ideally, this will be someone who knows you well, say your husband, wife, brother or sister, a long-term friend. But you and another unemployed executive might find it helpful to undertake a mutual self-help study, using each other as partners and critics.

This activity is *not* "make work." You're dealing with the rest of your life, and soul-searching is in order. As an older executive, it's especially important that you rethink your life goals and objectives. You're not the same person you were 10, 15, or even 30 years ago. You may be shocked to discover that you've been conducting your life on out-of-date, even archaic assumptions about yourself. Your time spent in getting reacquainted with yourself will be invaluable.

Make Valuable Contacts

Since it's been years since you've been job hunting, let's review briefly the importance of using your contacts. This is one area where you as an older executive should have a leg up on younger job seekers. You already *know* many people in your industry and have most likely developed a larger range of acquaintances and business associates.

As you're aware, two job markets exist, the *visible job market*, represented by jobs listed in newspaper advertisements, with state employment agencies, through executive recruiters, employment agencies, trade associations and college placement services; and the *invisible or hidden job market*, containing jobs which will soon be available due to retirements, expansion, understaffing, budget increases, or which might become available if the right person applied. These latter jobs are usually known to only a few people within an organization. Even the personnel departments are often unaware of their existence. At any given time, about 75 percent of the job potential is in this invisible market. Entry to this market is largely through personal contact (not what you know but who you know is often what counts here!).

Networking

In the early stages of your job search, you may not yet be aware of possible employment opportunities. You may have been so buried in your own job or situation that you haven't kept abreast of employment options in your industry or area of specialization. Your first inclination is to buy the Sunday paper and begin searching there. That's a valuable activity, but not as likely to be immediately productive as looking for information through the people you know. So, your initial task is to conduct a survey of the job market through their eyes.

Currently, formal networking has perhaps been overworked. What you'll be doing instead is simpler. Contact your friends and acquaintances to get whatever information they might have about the job situation. Ask them to give you the names of friends or acquaintances they have who might be willing to give you other information. Then use the first friends' and acquaintances' names as an entree to the next group of people. You're seeking information, not begging for a job.

At the beginning of the 1981 recession, "networking" as a deliberate employment strategy came heavily into vogue. (The principles have been around for years—networking is simply the development and use of business contacts.) Almost every major business publication had an article or articles on the efficacy of networking as a job hunting technique. But by the end of the recession in early 1984, networking had been overused by people who misunderstood its purpose and attempted to build up a phony network of new executive acquaintances who were supposed to have the open sesame to the job market. The result? Many executives who earlier were willing to help are no longer quite so open to networking contacts. Still, if you're careful and keep the time and scope of your contacts short, you should be able to elicit some useful information. Besides, you'll have recontacted a lot of people. When they find out you aren't going to be exploitative or attempt to "sweat them" for jobs, you'll rebuild some friendships. And you'll feel better just because you got out of the house and did something constructive.

Several guidelines are useful here:

□   Consider each contact as a resource whose time is valuable.
□   When you ask him or her for referrals, specify exactly what kind of organizations, departments, specialties or persons you'd like to be directed to.
□   Follow-up on the referrals you get. Then call or write back to your contacts to let them know what happened.
□   Be especially careful when friends have gone out on a limb to help you by arranging interviews with others. Go to the interviews prepared to meet new friends and to present yourself

in the best possible light as a worthy representative of your friends. One note of caution: since your friends may never have had to look for jobs, they may arrange some interviews which will be nonproductive from your standpoint. You still owe it to your friends to put your best foot forward so that you don't blow friendships by making them look bad.

□ Try to develop other possible leads from each new contact. However, don't press in such a way that he or she becomes uncomfortable.

□ Go to your meetings with each contact armed with a prepared list of questions you'd like answered. Keep the interviews short, thank the contact for talking with you, then leave.

□ Send each person a short and gracious thank-you note.

You may not find out the information you need on these initial visits. But you'll meet some nice people—and find that these meetings force you to think and to focus more closely on your employment goals and objectives.

According to Jane Wildman Raitt, writing in the article, "When Friendship Means Business," in *National Business Employment Weekly*, May 8, 1983, published by the *Wall Street Journal*, you have to answer three questions before networking will really function appropriately for you:

1. What kinds of contacts/referrals do I need to accomplish my new goals?

2. How many of my present contacts can help me achieve them?

3. How can I use my present network to create a new one that might furnish what I need?

Who do you contact? Develop a list of those people you think could provide you with additional contacts. Almost every older executive has at least 50 friends or acquaintances who might be helpful. Consider the following for starters:

□ Family members—father, mother, brothers, sisters, in-laws, aunts, uncles, cousins.

□ Friends from the past—co-workers from earlier jobs, neighbors, customers, military friends, fraternity or sorority members, former schoolmates.

□ People from your old job—employers or employees, fellow workers, competitors, salespeople, customers or clients.

□ People from your social contacts or organizations—church, synagogue, lodge or club members, sports groups—bowling, tennis, golf, sailing, hunting, etc.—hobby groups, contacts made through your children.

□ People whom you've contacted through charitable or public service groups.

□ Professionals who've provided services for you—bankers, lawyers, doctors, dentists, accountants, etc.

Business or Professional Organizations

You can make very useful contacts through the business or professional organizations that you either belong to or are eligible for. If you're a marketing executive, for example, you may have been paying dues for the Sales and Marketing Management Association, but not attending meetings. Or you may have felt that belonging to such organizations and going to meetings was a waste of time. In either event, change your tactics. Find out when and where the meetings are held, then go. You'll stay current in your profession or area of specialization, find out the latest in the field—and you may get important leads. Joining and paying your dues can be considered essential expenditures, and are tax deductible.

Job Search Organizations

Another excellent way to make contacts, get help writing your resumé, advice on setting up your job campaign and support in working your way through the emotional traumas of unemployment is to join a self-help organization for the unemployed executive or professional. There are a number of these around in various parts of the country, and they provide a very valuable service. But most do not focus on the special problems of the older out-of-work executive. However, a few organizations do provide services exclusively for the older executive. For instance, the 12 Forty Plus Clubs in the United States (there is even one in the United Kingdom) help only unemployed executives who are over 40. If one is in your area, you may find that it will provide the kind of support you need to get your job search campaign off the ground.[1]

Other Groups Which Might Help

State unemployment commissions rarely provide much in the way of help for the older executive and professional. But occasionally, their job counselors are able to provide leads or information on places you can get help. Since you have to go there anyway to collect your unemployment compensation, at least check out what help they might have, job opportunities they may know about or any other kind of assistance they can give.

In some cities, the Chamber of Commerce conducts Job Forums either alone or in conjunction with service organizations, sales executive clubs, advertising clubs or other such groups. These forums are usually free or charge a nominal fee. Consult your local chamber about availability.

Colleges and junior colleges frequently provide ongoing assistance to the unemployed through short courses (example: writing your resumé, interviewing) and counseling. Checking back with your own college or university placement bureau may be helpful (although these placement bureaus are generally geared toward recent graduates, in some disciplines they continue to be useful, e.g., education).

For women, CATALYST, Library and Career Planning Development, Inc., 14 East 60th Street, New York, NY 10022, has one of the most complete libraries on employment opportunities and career development anywhere. They also have current, up-to-date information on organizations providing assistance in all parts

---

1. A description of the way the Forty Plus Clubs operate, their addresses and those of other job search organizations are included in the appendix.

of the United States. They can be contacted in person, by mail, or by calling (212) 593-9700.

Recently, a number of organized religions have become concerned about the effect unemployment is having upon their adherents. In some areas, they are sponsoring self-help and/or counseling groups. These function primarily in a support role, giving members an opportunity to ventilate their fears and come to grips with feelings so they can learn better ways to cope with the pressures of unemployment. Call your local minister, priest or rabbi to see what, if anything, is available in your area. The YMCA, YWCA, YMHA and YWHA also provide similar services in some parts of the country.

You can also "let your fingers do the walking" by checking in the *Yellow Pages* for the listings under executive recruiters, management consultants, employment agencies, executive marketing and outplacement companies. These resources will be discussed in more detail later in this book.

Personal Communication Style
and How You Can
Make It Work for You

How you communicate with potential employers will ultimately determine your success in getting a job. It is also vital that you sell yourself so that others can see your abilities.

Unfortunately, three times out of four, you'll fail to do the best selling job, to convince the person with whom you're speaking, because you aren't using the way which is easiest for *them* to understand. In short, you'll communicate, but not as well as you're capable of doing. You'll fail to apply the communication golden rule which works just a little differently: "Thou shalt communicate with others in the manner through which *they* best understand." To apply this rule, you work at finding out their communication style, then deliver your communication in the manner people with that style understand best.

Communication Styles

As an older executive, you've been communicating with people for years. That's the name of the business game. And you may wonder why at this late date you need to know anything more about communication than you already do. Many reasons. Since communication *is* what much of business is about, the more you know about the way people communicate, the better off you'll be. You may not be aware of the vast array of differences in style because you peopled your division or department with clones who communicated in much the same way as you do. As a boss, that was your prerogative. Or, you have a whole raft of preconceptions and prejudices about people who communicate differently from you. You may distrust people who are glib and facile. You may have had a long-term running feud with salespeople or marketing people whom you felt were careless of facts or didn't pay enough attention to details. Or conversely, you may dislike people whom you feel are too concerned with detail and have difficulty communicating the big picture. At this late date, no one is going to try to revamp your own personal communication style. (That's impossible anyway, since it was probably set before you started school, as was the style of everyone with whom you come into contact.)[1]

For that reason, it's important for you to understand how you communicate and the way in which your communication style reflects your personality. During this period of time when you're out of work, it's useful to look objectively at yourself and to see that your communication style is OK. But now's the time to be flexible. Learn to spot potential employers' communication styles so that you can estimate the best way to approach them. Discover better ways to use your communications strengths and to modify those behaviors that can lead to problems with people communicating through other styles. And, learn how to sell yourself in ways that are acceptable to others and yet compatible with your feelings about yourself. In a nutshell: Don't try to make youself over. You can't. You have no choice but to retain the same basic communication style. But you can learn how to modify your presentation to match the preferred style of others.

Background of Communications Styles

A number of years ago, Dr. William Marston, a psychologist at Columbia University, studied "normal" behavior in people. He developed a system of identifying behaviors and related communications styles which is especially appropriate for the unemployed older executive.

By studying the way normal people reacted in all kinds of

---

1. The information in this section is adapted from copyrighted material developed by Jack Mohler, for Jack Mohler Associates, Garwood, NJ 07027-0153, and is used with Mr. Mohler's permission.

situations, Dr. Marston concluded that there were two sets of factors which interact to determine behavior. First is the environment: People exist in either a favorable or an unfavorable environment. (A neutral environment is not actively working against you, so has the same effect as a favorable environment.) Second is the way in which people react to that environment. They can react in only two ways. They can be active or they can be passive.

The environment can be represented as a continuum all the way from extremely unfavorable to highly favorable. People's reactions to those environments can also be represented as a continuum from highly active to extremely passive.

When these two factors are combined, four basic kinds of communications styles result. You can have active behavior in unfavorable environment or active behavior in a favorable environment. Similarly, you can be passive in an unfavorable environment or passive in a favorable environment. Figure 4.1 illustrates these four environments.

Basic Behaviors

In the top left-hand square, the environment is *unfavorable* or antagonistic, and the person in that environment is *active*. People who behave this way work to overcome the unfavorable conditions—to win, to dominate, to overcome. Their intent is to "dominate," and this behavior can be referred to as "High D." Those with "Low D" behavior react in the opposite way; they're so very meek that they never speak up and are counted. (For example: a male college friend who was so "Low D" that "a girl got him in trouble"!)

In the top right-hand quadrant, people are *active* in a *favorable* environment. Their behavior is outgoing, persuasive, gregarious. They love to communicate. They're very glib and facile with words. They convince and persuade. Their intent is to "influence." This behavior is called "High I" behavior. On the other hand, the person with "Low I" behavior would be very quiet and reserved—anything but outgoing.

In the lower right-hand quadrant, the environment is *favorable*,

Figure 4.1　William M. Marston's Four Factor Behavioral Model

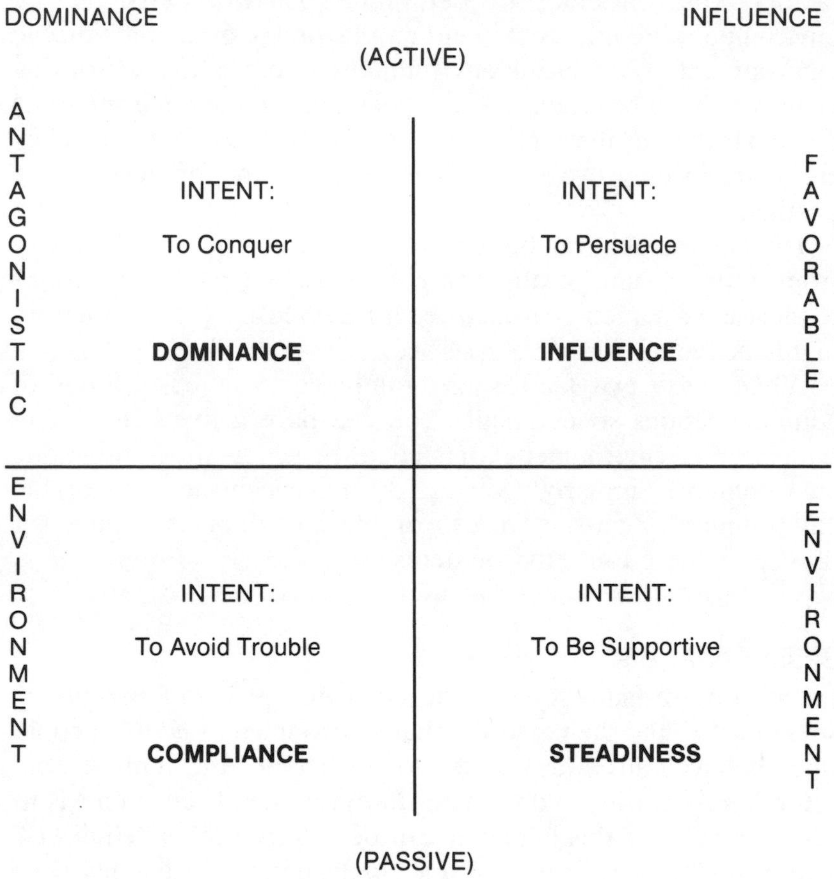

DOMINANCE　　　　　　　　　　　　　　　　　　INFLUENCE

(ACTIVE)

	DOMINANCE	INFLUENCE	
A N T A G O N I S T I C	INTENT: To Conquer **DOMINANCE**	INTENT: To Persuade **INFLUENCE**	F A V O R A B L E
E N V I R O N M E N T	INTENT: To Avoid Trouble **COMPLIANCE**	INTENT: To Be Supportive **STEADINESS**	E N V I R O N M E N T

(PASSIVE)

but the people whose behavior puts them in this quadrant tend to be *passive*. They're friendly, but in a low-key way. They prefer to sit back, work quietly, but steadily, and provide support. They like to be thought of as steady and reliable—and they communicate in this way. The intent is to be supportive, and this behavior is, accordingly, called "High S." By way of contrast, the opposite behavior, "Low S," would be high gear, fast moving, could be erratic, or at least sporadic, and would prefer a lot of different kinds of activities.

The final way in which people respond is found in the lower left-hand quadrant. In this unfavorable environment, the people respond passively; they follow the roles and do things right because it keeps them out of trouble. They're very careful what they say, they're concerned about facts and details. They conform to what is expected of them. This style of behavior is referred to as "High C" behavior, and the intent is to conform. "Low C" behavior, on the other hand, is nonconformist and independent.

But you may say, "I behave differently at different times. I can see myself at times in each of those quadrants." Yes, that's true. Everyone is an interesting and different mix of behaviors from all four quadrants. You may be very high in one quadrant and be very low in another. But for a short period of time, you could behave in the manner appropriate to that quadrant if it would be helpful to you to do so.

You can probably already see why this way of looking at behavior might be valuable to you. Being unemployed is certainly existing in a most unfavorable and difficult environment. And it is for that very reason why unemployed people frequently fail to present themselves in the best light. They perceive that they are in an unfavorable environment and communicate in a manner appropriate to that environment. But interviewers, for example, may think they're in a favorable environment. You need to communicate with them in a manner that matches *their* current perceptions.

Now, it's time for you to find out how you stack up in each of these quadrants. Figure 4.2 contains a list of 24 sets of four words. Each of these sets of four words represents a group of behaviors. For each set of four words, choose the one word which is most like you, and place an X in the M column. Then choose the one word from the remaining three which is least like the way you normally behave, and put an X in the L column. Continue in the same way through all 24 sets of words. Be sure to check back when you finish to see that you made one choice only for the word *most* like you and one choice only for the word *least* like you for each set of words.

In any given situation, you will react according to the way you perceive the environment. If you perceive that the environment is unfavorable or antagonistic, and you are generally active in an unfavorable environment, you'll exhibit the characteristics of High

Figure 4.2

Personal Concept

READ CAREFULLY: In the three columns below there are eight four-word groups. Select two words in each group--one which is MOST like you and one which is LEAST like you. Use an (X) to mark your choices.

	M	L
EXAMPLE: AUTOCRATIC	X	
CONGENIAL		
STABLE		X
EXACTING		

	M	L			M	L			M	L
EXPRESSIVE				HIGH-SPIRITED				ADVENTUROUS		
COMPLIANT				TALKATIVE				ENTHUSIASTIC		
FORCEFUL				GOOD-NATURED				ADAPTABLE		
RESTRAINED				SOFTSPOKEN				LOYAL		
FORCE-OF-CHARACTER				CONTENTED				HUMBLE		
CAREFUL				IMPATIENT				GOOD LISTENER		
EMOTIONAL				CONVINCING				ENTERTAINING		
SATISFIED				RESIGNED				WILL POWER		
CORRECT				RESPECTFUL				LIFE-OF-THE-PARTY		
PIONEERING				GOOD MIXER				OBEDIENT		
EASY MARK				AGGRESSIVE				TOLERANT		
INFLUENTIAL				GENTLE				COMPETITIVE		
PRECISE				POISED				CAUTIOUS		
DOMINEERING				CONVENTIONAL				NEIGHBORLY		
WILLING				NERVY				VIGOROUS		
ATTRACTIVE				ACCOMMODATING				PERSUASIVE		
EVEN-TEMPERED				CONFIDENT				RESERVED		
STIMULATING				COOPERATIVE				OUTSPOKEN		
FUSSY				ARGUMENTATIVE				STRICT		
DETERMINED				RELAXED				ELOQUENT		
TIMID				RESTLESS				OBLIGING		
DEMANDING				WELL-DISCIPLINED				ANIMATED		
PATIENT				INSPIRING				DOGGED		
CAPTIVATING				CONSIDERATE				DEVOUT		
OPEN-MINDED				DIPLOMATIC				ASSERTIVE		
COMPANIONABLE				COURAGEOUS				GREGARIOUS		
KIND				SYMPATHETIC				NONCHALANT		
SELF-RELIANT				OPTIMISTIC				DOCILE		
AGREEABLE				EAGER				OUTGOING		
SELF-CONTROLLED				POSITIVE				BOLD		
PLAYFUL				LENIENT				MODERATE		
PERSISTENT				GOD-FEARING				PERFECTIONIST		

D behavior and communicate very aggressively. You may end up antagonizing people. If you tend to react passively, though, you may be so low key and unassertive that you could end up failing to make any impression at all. But while you're reacting, other people are also reacting and communicating according to their perceptions of the environment. Your perceptions may be diametrically opposed!

Specifically, spend enough time observing the situation in an interview to make an accurate judgment about how the interviewer views the environment and which behavior quadrant he or she is operating in at the time. Then, match your presentation to that style.

To do that, you need to know more about each style, the characteristics you can observe, and the method of communication that works best for each.

HIGH D

Behaviors: High D people are self-starters who get going when things get tough. They thrive on both challenge and competition. They are direct, positive and straightforward. They say what they think and can be very blunt and to the point.

They like to be on center stage—they are take charge people. They fight hard for what they think is the way to go, but can accept defeat and don't hold grudges.

They prefer variety, the unusual, the adventurous. And they will lose interest if their jobs become routine, so they must constantly be involved. They are prone to make job changes, especially early in their careers, but when they find the challenge they need, they'll stay.

They are individualistic and self-sufficient. They demand a lot of both themselves and others. They are discontented and dissatisfied with the status quo.

How they appear: They will probably be running late. They can be or appear to be rude. They will interrupt you, take phone calls, read letters, call to their secretaries or otherwise interrupt you as you are talking. (Go ahead, I'm listening.) Their offices or desks may appear disorganized, with stacks of papers sitting around. The key to recognizing the High D person is his impulsiveness and impatience. Dress may or may not be a clue. If they also tend to be active in a favorable environment (High I characteristics), they will be well dressed. But if they are low in I characteristics, they probably don't care much about their external appearance, so may be sloppy, or at least unstylish. A messy office, careless dress and sloppy grooming is a dead giveaway that the person is a High D.

How to communicate with people showing High D characteristics: They want you to be brief (remember, they're "bottom-line" people), so get to the point quickly. Stress what you can do for them or for their company. They want you to be sure of yourself, so be firm, don't pussyfoot around. Level with them. They'll act on impulse, so hit them quickly and hard—but not argumentatively. In short, communicate with them in the same manner which they project.

Many top executives exhibit High D tendencies. You may be one yourself, or remember a few from your old job. Your interviews with them will be short, to the point. They'll leave the details for someone else to fill in.

HIGH I

Behaviors: High I people are outgoing, persuasive and gregarious. They strive to persuade others and make their opinions and beliefs prevail. High I people are very comfortable in "one-on-one" situations. Their outgoing nature and the image they project is that of the so-called "natural salesperson."

High I people are basically interested in other people. They are poised and meet strangers easily—and people respond easily to them. They inherently trust and accept people, and are incurably optimistic. For that reason, they may misjudge people's abilities and intentions, with occasional disastrous results.

They are easy conversationalists, doing everything they can to put others at ease. They sell themselves well. In business, they are friendly competitors and optimistic, though not too well-organized managers.

High I people normally dress very fashionably, in the latest "in" style. They join organizations for prestige and for personal recognition. They usually have a broad range of acquaintances and tend to "name-drop."

How they appear: Their ego is apt to be all over the office. There will be pictures of *them* getting awards, plaques with *their* names on them, certificates, trophies and so on. You will know exactly who occupies that office. They will be friendly, outgoing, enthusiastic. And, of course, their dress is a good clue. Above all, the key to recognizing High I people is their egos. You will hear this because they talk constantly, using the word "I"—"I did this, I did that." They will tell you how wonderful they are, how wonderful their company is and so forth.

How to communicate with people with High I characteristics: They like the special, the novel—if it's new, it's exciting. Since they like to talk about themselves, let them tell you about what they've been doing. Don't attempt to dominate the conversation. (You couldn't anyway—they'd interrupt you.) They want to be the first to do something and, above all, they want recognition. Emphasize the ways in which you can help them get what they want, the recognition they want (and need). Compliment them (sincerely) on their office, their organization, whatever. Use a broad brush in telling them about your accomplishments and omit the details. Details are boring to High I's.

A number of High I executives have made it to or near the top, especially in sales and marketing, public relations, advertising and people-intensive businesses. You may very well have had a few on staff at your old job.

HIGH S
Behaviors: High S people are usually amiable, easygoing and relaxed. Most of the time, they are even-tempered, low-key and unobtrusive. They hate to be singled out in a crowd. They tend to be complacent, are frequently lenient with others, but emotionally mature.

They are warmhearted, love their homes and are excellent neighbors. They work at being a friend and probably have the same friends they made years ago.

They tend to be undemonstrative and controlled. They conceal their feelings from others—and they hold grudges. The saying, "I don't get mad, I get even," is very true for the High S.

High S individuals strive to keep things the way they are and dislike change. Once underway, they work steadily and patiently. They dislike urgency and the pressure of deadlines.

They seldom argue or openly criticize, but can quietly resist and slow things down. They're passive resisters normally but, pushed to the wall, can be implacable enemies.

They tend to be very possessive and develop strong attachments for things, family, co-workers, their departments and companies.

How they appear: They will be very low key. Their dress will most likely be conservative and neat. Their offices will also be neat, but not compulsively so. They will have only one or no more than a few papers or folders on their desks. The pictures in their offices will be of their possessions—their spouses, their families, their houses, boats, airplanes, summer cottages and so on. Their possessiveness is usually evident in nameplates on both the desk and door. They may also have labeled their staplers, Scotch tape dispensers and other objects on the desk or in the room. Don't touch any of them—they may resent it. They will appear to be very easygoing, but are very security-conscious.

If you don't see anything in their behavior or in their office that identified them as High D, High I, or High C, they're most likely High S people, and you can make that as a tentative identification.

How to communicate with people with High S tendencies: Sell yourself first, in a low-key, nondramatic way. You must win them as friends, then they'll go along with you as a friend. Don't move too fast at first, they may resent it. (The High D has the most trouble with a High S. High D pushiness may cause the High S to react negatively.) Let them move at their own pace. Don't push or hurry them. They may resent it and get their back up (which you wouldn't know because they are masters at hiding their feelings) and you will have blown the interview. Talk security, service, dependability and backup. Don't talk about turnarounds, instituting changes, etc. These are threatening. They expect you to take a sincere personal interest in them and their company. Provide all the details they want and be prepared to answer their questions fully. Don't attempt to take over the interview to try to move it ahead. They'll get where they're going in their own good time.

More High S people are middle managers than top-level executives, and you're likely to find them in personnel departments. *You must get past these people before you can hope to get a job.*

HIGH C

Behaviors: High C individuals are characterized by orderliness. They are precise and attentive to detail. They strive for a neat, orderly existence and tend to follow traditional procedures and established systems. They are reserved, conservative, adaptable, open-minded (to a point) and diplomatic. They are careful with people because they stay out of trouble that way. They prefer to adapt to situations and to compromise, if necessary, to avoid conflict and antagonism. They try very hard to stay out of hot water and to avoid stepping on toes. They tend to document everything they do.

They are naturally cautious and tentative in decision-making. When they are convinced by fact and detail, they will make up their mind and may be very rigid should change be necessary. They try very hard to be what others want and expect them to be. They have high personal standards and try to live up to them. They expect others also to meet the same high standards they set for themselves.

How they appear: Their offices will be neat and orderly. Their desks will be clean and they will appear to be unhurried. If there are pictures in the office, they will probably be of things—landscapes, still lifes, abstracts or attractive photographs. They will be prepared for your visit, will be on time and will have read your letters, resumé and/or job application. They'll be courteous and diplomatic, but will have detailed, precise questions to ask. They will be dressed conservatively and will almost always be very well groomed.

How to communicate with people with High C tendencies: Be

precise and technically correct—don't generalize. Be sure you answer all the questions carefully and completely. Use many facts and include the how's and why's, if they ask. They're interested in research, statistics, facts and details. Supply all the details they want, but don't get caught trying to manipulate the facts and figures in your favor. The key is recognizing the precise manner of High C managers and that they organize everything. So organize your answers accordingly.

Because they are cautious, avoid telling them about the massive changes you made on your last job unless you set the framework first. Talk in detail about the research and preparation that it took before you could make such a far-reaching change. Their extreme caution makes them want quality, reliability and precedent. Show how you followed the rules and helped your employers reach their stated goals. If you leave a resumé, give them one which includes a full listing of prior job responsibilities.

Determining Your Style

The answers you gave on the quiz you took in Figure 4.2 can be used to develop a profile that tells you how high or how low you are on each of the sets of characteristics. You can place these answers on a chart and have a picture that represents generally how you'll come across to others when you communicate. A sample profile might look something like Figure 4.3.

Now, check your answers to find out which of the quadrants you score high in and which you score low in. Look at the list in Figure 4.4. For each group of four words, one word represented a D action, one an I, one an S and one a C. Go back to the answers you marked on Figure 4.2. Next to each M answer and each L answer, write the letter (D, I, S or C) corresponding to the quadrant that answer represents.

Next, count the D responses you made in the M column and put that total in the box marked D in the center of figure 4.5 under the M column. Repeat your count for the I answers, the S and the D. Add the number of responses you counted to see that you had 24. If not, go back and recount to find out what you omitted.

Figure 4.3. Sample Profile

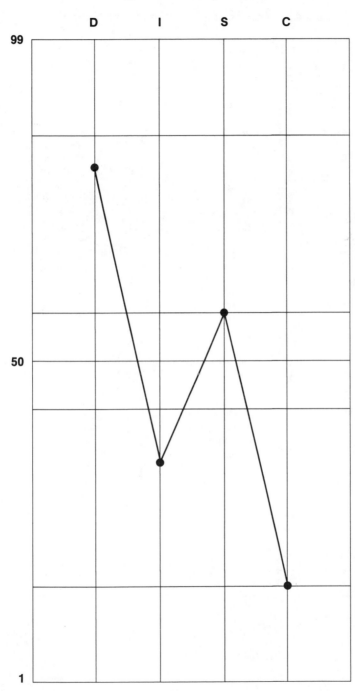

Figure 4.4. Answer Key Communications Styles Quiz

EXPRESSIVE	I	HIGH-SPIRITED	D	ADVENTUROUS	D
COMPLIANT	C	TALKATIVE	I	ENTHUSIASTIC	I
FORCEFUL	D	GOOD-NATURED	S	ADAPTABLE	C
RESTRAINED	S	SOFTSPOKEN	C	LOYAL	S
•		•		•	
FORCE-OF-CHARACTER	D	CONTENTED	S	HUMBLE	C
CAREFUL	C	IMPATIENT	D	GOOD LISTENER	S
EMOTIONAL	I	CONVINCING	I	ENTERTAINING	I
SATISFIED	S	RESIGNED	C	WILL POWER	D
•		•		•	
CORRECT	C	RESPECTFUL	C	LIFE-OF-THE-PARTY	I
PIONEERING	D	GOOD MIXER	I	OBEDIENT	S
EASY MARK	S	AGGRESSIVE	D	TOLERANT	C
INFLUENTIAL	I	GENTLE	S	COMPETITIVE	D
•		•		•	
PRECISE	C	POISED	I	CAUTIOUS	C
DOMINEERING	D	CONVENTIONAL	C	NEIGHBORLY	S
WILLING	S	NERVY	D	VIGOROUS	D
ATTRACTIVE	I	ACCOMMODATING	S	PERSUASIVE	I
•		•		•	
EVEN-TEMPERED	S	CONFIDENT	I	RESERVED	S
STIMULATING	I	COOPERATIVE	C	OUTSPOKEN	D
FUSSY	C	ARGUMENTATIVE	D	STRICT	C
DETERMINED	D	RELAXED	S	ELOQUENT	I
•		•		•	
TIMID	C	RESTLESS	D	OBLIGING	S
DEMANDING	D	WELL-DISCIPLINED	C	ANIMATED	I
PATIENT	S	INSPIRING	I	DOGGED	D
CAPTIVATING	I	CONSIDERATE	S	DEVOUT	C
•		•		•	
OPEN-MINDED	C	DIPLOMATIC	C	ASSERTIVE	D
COMPANIONABLE	I	COURAGEOUS	D	GREGARIOUS	I
KIND	S	SYMPATHETIC	S	NONCHALANT	S
SELF-RELIANT	D	OPTIMISTIC	I	DOCILE	C
•		•		•	
AGREEABLE	C	EAGER	I	OUTGOING	I
SELF-CONTROLLED	S	POSITIVE	D	BOLD	D
PLAYFUL	I	LENIENT	S	MODERATE	S
PERSISTENT	D	GOD-FEARING	C	PERFECTIONIST	C

Figure 4.5.   Personal Concept Scoring Form—Communication Style

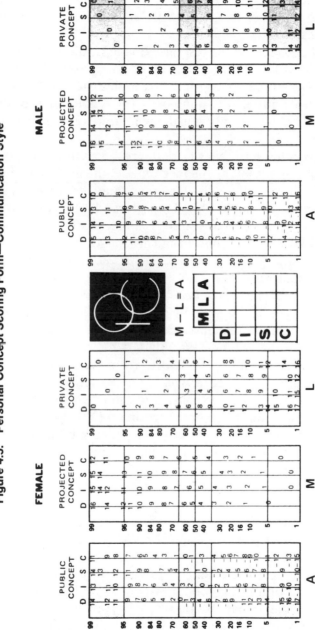

Repeat the counting procedure for the responses you made in the L column. Count the D, I, S and C responses you made and put them in the box in figure 4.5 under the L heading. They should total 24 responses.

Then, subtract the responses in the L column from the number in the M column to find the difference between the two. Put that number in the appropriate box under the A heading. You'll have positive and negative numbers in the A column if you did it right. To check: add the numbers in the A column together. They should total zero.

Note that on either side of figure 4.5 are three sets of graphs. The graphs on the left are headed female, the graphs on the right, male. You can use either the male or female set of graphs—whichever you're comfortable with! The left-hand graph in each set is marked *public concept* above and A underneath. The center graph is marked *projected concept* and has the letter M underneath, and the right-hand graph is labeled *private concept* and has the letter L underneath.

Transfer the scores from the M column onto the center graph in the set you're using and circle the corresponding number. If the number of the response you made isn't on the graph, interpolate between the two nearest numbers.

Similarly, transfer the scores from the L column onto the right-hand graph marked *private concept* and the scores from the A column onto the left-hand graph marked *public concept*.

Finally, join the scores together—D to I to S to C—to get the profiles representing your communication behaviors.

So far, so good. But what do those three profiles mean? Basically, your M responses and the projected concepts profile indicate the way you think you should act and communicate to be successful. This profile is heavily influenced by your general economic situation, your last job, your family, etc. It can also show the stresses you are placing on yourself to try to accomplish your objectives.

Your L responses and the private concepts profile reflect the way you respond when you know people well or are in the privacy of your home. It may also represent the way you respond when you are severely stressed and your projected concepts "mask" slips.

The public concepts profile and the A set of numbers represent what the public sees—and reflects the interaction between the concept of yourself you're projecting and the way you communicate and behave in private.

Most people have strengths in two of the quadrants. For example, in Figure 4.6, this person has a primary strength in the S or steadiness quadrant and a secondary strength in the C or compliance quadrant. Both behaviors are passive. This person will exhibit the behavior of the S quadrant in a favorable environment and will communicate in the C style in an unfavorable environment.

Almost an exact opposite behavior is that exhibited by the person with the profile shown in Figure 4.7. This person is active in both the unfavorable and favorable environments, exhibiting High D behavior in the unfavorable and High I in the favorable. Interestingly enough, in business a person communicating in High S or High C styles will have a terrible time communicating with someone behaving in a High D or High I mode unless both make adjustments in style and are aware of and respect the differences in style. (In marriage, however, opposites really do attract, and High D people often marry High S people, and a High I will often marry a High C. That way, they cover all the territories. What one can't do the other can.)

To read the strengths and possible weaknesses of your own pattern, transfer the public concept profile (the left-hand profile) you developed in Figure 4.5 onto both the probable strengths and the possible weaknesses graphs in Figure 4.8. The shaded portions of the graphs are in the same relative positions. Use these and the percentile markings at the side to approximate the profile positions. Begin on the D column, then continue on to the I, the S and the C columns. Using the center of the graph (marked with the numeral 50) as the starting point, you can read your probable strengths and weaknesses this way: if the marking is above 50, read all the words from 50 up to and including the charted point; if the marking is below 50, read all the words from 50 down to and including the charted point. This list of words describes the way you might appear to people who like you (probable strengths) and people who don't like you (possible weaknesses).

Figure 4.6
PUBLIC CONCEPT

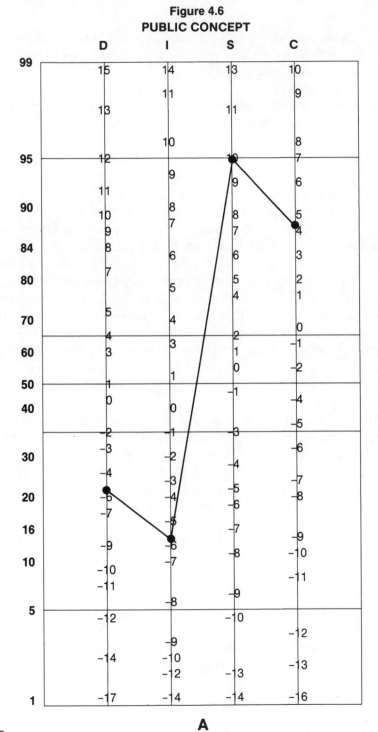

A

Figure 4.7
PUBLIC CONCEPT

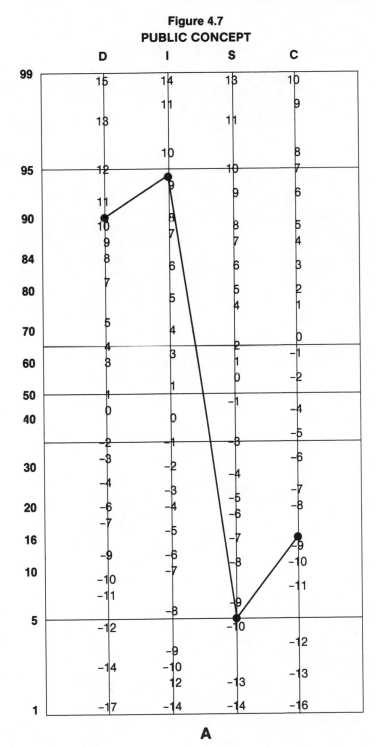

A

Figure 4.8
PUBLIC CONCEPT
PROBABLE STRENGTHS

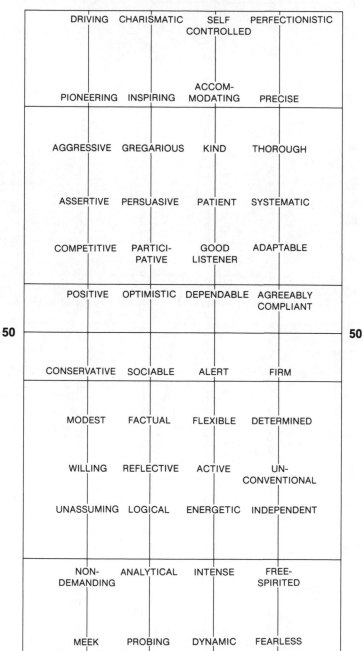

	D	I	S	C
	DRIVING	CHARISMATIC	SELF CONTROLLED	PERFECTIONISTIC
	PIONEERING	INSPIRING	ACCOM-MODATING	PRECISE
	AGGRESSIVE	GREGARIOUS	KIND	THOROUGH
	ASSERTIVE	PERSUASIVE	PATIENT	SYSTEMATIC
	COMPETITIVE	PARTICI-PATIVE	GOOD LISTENER	ADAPTABLE
	POSITIVE	OPTIMISTIC	DEPENDABLE	AGREEABLY COMPLIANT
50	CONSERVATIVE	SOCIABLE	ALERT	FIRM
	MODEST	FACTUAL	FLEXIBLE	DETERMINED
	WILLING	REFLECTIVE	ACTIVE	UN-CONVENTIONAL
	UNASSUMING	LOGICAL	ENERGETIC	INDEPENDENT
	NON-DEMANDING	ANALYTICAL	INTENSE	FREE-SPIRITED
	MEEK	PROBING	DYNAMIC	FEARLESS

50

Figure 4.8
PUBLIC CONCEPT
POSSIBLE WEAKNESSES

D	I	S	C
BELLIGERENT	SELF PROMOTING	PHLEGMATIC	OVERLY DEPENDENT
DICTATORIAL	SUPERFICIAL	INDIF-FERENT	EVASIVE
ARROGANT	OVERLY OPTIMISTIC	TOO LENIENT	WORRISOME
DEMANDING	GLIB	POSSESSIVE	DEFENSIVE
NERVY	OVERLY-CONFIDENT	COM-PLACENT	NIT PICKER
HASTY	POOR LISTENER	NON-DEMON-STRATIVE	TOO-COMPLIANT

50   50

D	I	S	C
HESITANT	RESERVED	RESTLESS	OPINIONATED
SHY	BLUNT	IMPATIENT	STUBBORN
OVER-CAUTIOUS	SUSPICIOUS	PUSHY	IMMOVABLE
HUMBLE	ALOOF	TENSE	REBELLIOUS
FEARFUL	PESSIMISTIC	IMPETUOUS	DEFIANT
INTIMIDATED	WITHDRAWN	HYPER-ACTIVE	RADICAL

If you've done everything according to directions so far, you should have a profile of your overall style with which you will pretty much agree. One further note: When the projected concepts profile is radically different from the private concept, the public concept may not give a completely true picture of your basic self. You may want to try overlaying the private concept profile on the charts in Figure 4.8 as a check on what your style would be without the added stresses of the concept you're attempting to project.

Since most people's basic styles are set during childhood, it's very difficult to make a substantive change in style. What's far easier to handle, though, is to find out what behaviors in the different quadrants most heavily impact on others and modify those on a situation-by-situation basis.

For example:

High D   Are impatient. Don't give others an opportunity to think and to assimilate. Tend to be impulsive, to blow up when things go wrong, but get over their anger fast. (This is a disaster with a High S. The High S will brood about it and not get over his feelings.) Fail to consult or share. One-way communication—tell, not ask. Poor listeners. May not be sensitive to feelings and needs of others. May try to dominate and override others, or intimidate them. Too blunt. Most difficult style to relate to: High S.

High I   Too global—find detail difficult. May act without thinking. May be too superficial, too optimistic. Frequently too talky and don't give other people an opportunity to respond. Like people and may trust too much. Give poor directions. May not listen enough and may cut others off because they don't respond fast enough. Tend to "wing it," go off on tangents. May be too outgoing, too effervescent. Most difficult style to relate to: High C.

High S   Slow to respond. May be seen as too indirect, as lacking conviction or not forceful enough. May spend too much time on tasks and lack sense of urgency. May be too patient, spend too much time listening and not enough asking or telling. May be stubborn or clam up when pushed. Most difficult style to relate to: High D. (They feel too pushed and threatened by the High D style.)

High C May talk too deliberately, concentrate too much on details and the "small" picture. Everything must be in exactly the right form, which others may view as picky. May move too slowly and cautiously. Want things written rather than told. Will ask (and ask) rather than tell. May be too sensitive to possible slights, yet critical of faults in others. Most difficult style to relate to: High I.

Determining Personal Stress

Unemployment is obviously a time of considerable stress for everyone, including older executives. Anything you can do to lessen your internal stress will make it easier for you to concentrate on the important elements of your job search.

In making your choices for your communications style, you have already shown whether you are stressing yourself in the communications area. By determining the differences between the respective M and L scores, you can find out whether you are placing yourself under minimum, average or high levels of stress.[1]

Example: In Figure 4.9 are one unemployed executive's M and L profiles. At the left of each profile is a column of figures representing the percentile rankings of the various scores.

Look at the D scores first. On the M profile, the D percentile is 84, while on the L profile, it's about 46, a difference of 38 points. On the I scale, the M percentile is about 55, the L, about 75, a difference of 20 points. The S difference is 20 points (30 and 10), and the C difference is 12 points (48 and 36). The total points of stress:

$$D + I + S + C = \text{Points of Stress}$$
$$38 + 20 + 20 + 12 = 90 \text{ points}$$

---

1. No doubt by now you have identified the scoring process as a variation of the Bell curve of distribution. The middle-shaded portion on each profile represents the "averages"—those scores within one standard deviation from the mean, while the outside shaded portions represent the extremes on the scores.

Figure 4.9. Stress Points.

MALE
PROJECTED CONCEPT

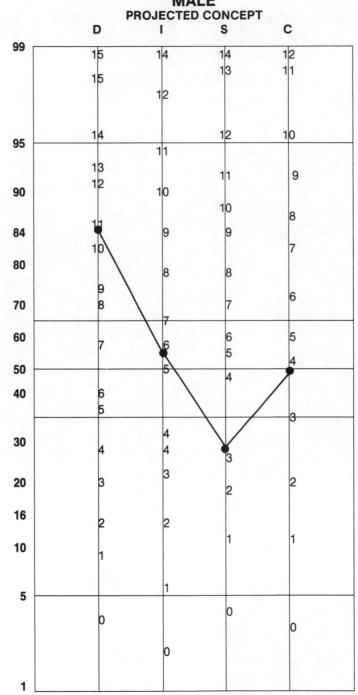

M

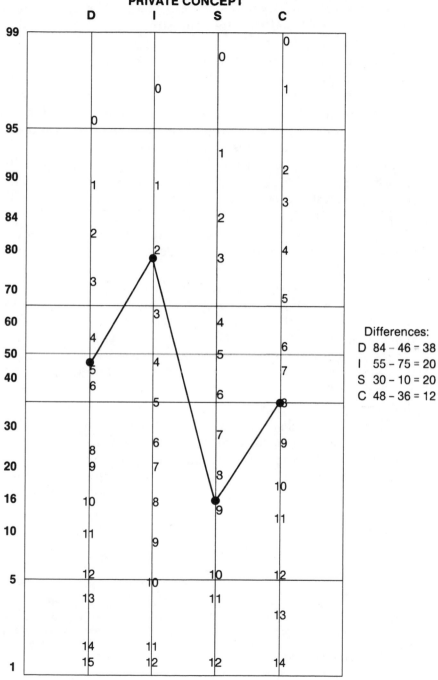

Figure 4.9.   Stress Points.
MALE
PRIVATE CONCEPT

Differences:
D 84 – 46 = 38
I   55 – 75 = 20
S 30 – 10 = 20
C 48 – 36 = 12

Generally speaking, anywhere between 0 and 40 points is minimum stress, between 41 and 80, moderate stress, and above 81, high stress.

To explain what kinds of stress this executive is placing on himself: He feels that to be successful, he must be aggressive and assertive, so he pushes this aspect of his personality—which is already in the "average" range. (Incidentally, pushing D characteristics higher is difficult—and almost impossible for those people whose basic D scores are in the low range.)

But what he is doing with his I characteristics is especially revealing. In this instance, he basically is an outgoing person who really likes people. But to be successful, he feels that he should hold back on this behavior. Almost invariably an attempt to lessen an outreach to people represents bitter experience: the individual trusted someone or more than one person too much and was disappointed.

The change in the S scale is one that executives often try to make. This executive has an extremely low S rating, which generally reflects a perception of time. He probably moves quickly to get things done and is very active. But the higher rating in the M profile suggests that he is trying to be more patient, to be less demanding of the people he's managing. He's trying to cut down on his expectations that people "get things done yesterday." (Sometimes, this increase in the S may simply mean that an unemployed person is trying to deal realistically with the fact that getting a job takes time—and he or she can't control the process.)

Finally, the C changes may tell either or both of two things: he is trying to become less independent (the higher the C score, the greater the dependence) and/or he is trying to pay more attention to details to be sure that nothing falls through the cracks.[1]

---

1. Note: For a fuller explanation of your individual communications style than is possible in this chapter, send photocopies of Figure 4.2, Personal Concept, and Figure 5.2, Position Concept (in the next chapter), showing your responses, along with a check or money order for $5.00 to Jack Mohler Associates, Box 153, Garwood, NJ 07027-0153.

Making Adaptations in
Style to Match Job Search Requirements

As you begin your job search, evaluate the communications styles of the people you meet. Make guesses about the best way to interact with people that are not connected to your job search. Try to communicate with both groups according to your judgment of their style. Then ask yourself: Were you right? Was your interaction easier?

You'll find your judgments get better as you go. Practice does make perfect. In any event, by tuning in to their words, actions and surroundings, and paying attention to them as individuals, your communication will be more rewarding. Why? Because your attention is outward toward them, and not inward, toward yourself.

You'll also want to use different styles of resumés, different kinds of letters, and different ways of interacting in interviews, based on your judgments about styles. Those adaptations will be discussed in later chapters.

What Kind of Job
Should You Search For?

If you completed the exercises in the last section, you have a good idea of your skills, strengths and weaknesses, goals and objectives and so on. But you still may not know what kind of job you are best suited for or what kind of job to search for.

Part of this is related to your personality. It's more comfortable and less effort to look for a job in areas(s) in which you've already worked. Radically changing job types is a great personal risk. Can you face the risk you'd have to take to start a second (or even third) career at your age? Or should you stay in the same kind of job because you personally aren't constituted to risk that much?

Harry Levinson, a well-known industrial psychologist, writes frequently on career topics and career changes. In the May/June 1983 issue of the *Harvard Business Review*, he points out that:

> The most critical factor for people to consider in choosing a gratifying second career is their ego ideal. It can serve as a road map. Central to a person's aspirations, the ego ideal is an idealized image of oneself in the future. It includes the goals people would like to achieve and how they would like to see themselves . . .

> Throughout life people strive toward their ego ideal, but no one ever achieves it. With successive accomplishments, aspirations rise. But as people feel they are progressing toward their ego ideal, their self-pictures are more rather than less positive. The closer people get to their ego ideal, therefore, the better they feel about themselves. The

71

greater the gap between one's ego ideal and one's current self-image, the angrier one is at oneself and the more inadequate, guilty and depressed one feels.

When a career helps satisfy the ego ideal, life and work are rewarding and enjoyable. When a career does not help meet these self-demands, work is a curse. In short, the wish to attain the ego ideal, to like oneself, is the most powerful of motivating forces. Delivery on the promises one makes to oneself is an important aspect of choosing a new direction.

What Is Your Ego Ideal?

Levinson suggests that reviewing your family history, school and work experiences can help you to outline the needs that are critical to your ego ideal. Answering the following eight sets of questions will help you to know your ego ideals and give you a sense of the main thrust of your life.

1. What were your father's or father-substitute's values? Not what did your father say or do, but what did he stand for? What things were important to him? What was the code he lived by? Similarly, analyze your mother's values.
2. What was the first thing you did that pleased your mother? (This is important because usually the first person that children try to please is their mother. Later, pleasing their father becomes important, too.) For women, the mother's values system may have more weight in forming their values (question 1), with the activities they did to please a parent (question 2) being performed with the father in mind. These two questions should give you insight into the way you formed the base for your current values system.
3. Who were your childhood heroes or heroines? Did you idolize athletes, movie stars, or political figures? What kind of people do you now enjoy reading about or watching on TV? What kind of achievements do you admire?
4. Who are and were your models—relatives, teachers, scoutmasters, preachers, bosses, characters in stories? What did they say or do that made you admire them?
5. When you were able to make choices, what were they? What

major did you pursue in college? What jobs have you accepted? (These may appear to be random, but they were not. Look at them carefully to find the pattern.)

6. What few experiences in your lifetime have been the most gratifying? Which gave you the greatest pleasure and sense of elation? The pleasure you took in the experience was really the pleasure you took in yourself. What were you doing?

7. Of all the things you've done, at which were you the most successful? What were you doing and how were you doing it?

8. What would you like your epitaph or obituary to say? What would you like to be remembered for? What would you like to leave as a memorial?

After you complete your answers, review your occupational activities to determine those that fit the way you like to behave—to do your job or deal with your co-workers. Ask yourself, "In what environment am I comfortable?"

Try discussing your answers to these questions with a friend. During your discussion, also explore these other areas of your personality:

□ How do you handle aggressive energy? Do you channel it into the organization and administration of projects or do you bottle it up?
□ How do you handle affection? Do you enjoy interacting with others or do you feel more comfortable keeping your distance? Can you express your emotions to others? (Thank them, praise them, give them a pat on the back?)
□ How do you handle dependency? Can you make decisions or do you honestly prefer that someone else make them? Do you want to be in charge, be a team member or work independently?

You are really trying to answer for yourself, "Do I want to continue as manager—or would I have a better life with less frustration doing something else?" If the answer is *yes*, ask yourself what that something else should be. The last question is one of the soul-searchers of all time. You are asking yourself to start over, or at least, to enter uncharted territory.

After serious reflection, if you discover that you really don't want to leave the field in which you've been working to start a new career, you still have a number of other questions to answer.

- Where do you want to look (locale)? Are you willing to relocate? (Before you can answer that one honestly, you must discuss this thoroughly with your family, since their desires have to be considered in such a momentous decision. Particularly with the two-career family, the question of "where" becomes crucial to a successful job search.)
- What size company do you want to work for? Fortune 500 or small business or industry?
- Should you look for a management position, or are you willing to accept a lesser position if the long-term prospects look good?
- Are you willing to "settle," to accept almost any job, just so it is interesting and will last long enough for you to reach retirement age?

Still not ready to make a decision or you don't yet have enough direction? Read on. By the time you complete the exercises in the following pages, you should know enough about yourself to decide whether to change or look for more of the same.

Matching Communication Styles and Jobs

When people plan their careers, they are generally attracted to job areas and professions which match in some way their communication styles. As they advance in business, however, the job demands are different, and different communications styles are needed. Managers succeed or fail on the basis of their ability to adapt—to match their communication styles to the requirements of their jobs.

Job Areas

In essence, this means that jobs, like people, have "personalities" and communications needs. The managerial positions you want and are qualified for demand that you make constant minor (or major) adjustments to your basic style. That's a given for success when you're managing people. You'll be happier—and better able to make the needed adjustments—if you understand whether you have a natural fit for the job (and must make only minor situational adjustments in style) or whether you must constantly watch for situations where you'll have to make major adjustments in your style.

Figure 5.1 is an illustration showing how careers fit into the four DISC quadrants. It shows some of the major jobs that are compatible with the different kinds of communication styles. Beginning with the D quadrant: The positions in the bottom portion of the quadrant are high D positions in which some measure of high C would be valuable. In the top part of the quadrant are positions requiring High D behaviors with a lesser measure of High I style. Over the line into the top of the I quadrant are the positions for which High I behavior, pushed by a lesser High D, are helpful. These positions are frequently in the sales area. High I positions which call upon for some measure of supportive High S behavior are shown in the bottom part of the sector. In the High S quadrant, the jobs shown in the top of the quadrant are High S jobs requiring occasional outgoing High I behaviors. The bottom of the segment shows the High S jobs which have a High C component-positions in which services are provided. On into the High C sector are first the positions requiring High C attention to detail along with some High S supportive behaviors. And finally, at the bottom of the C quadrant are shown those positions that require High C attention to detail, but also some assertiveness and overcoming of obstacles.

You can determine the personality of the job you're looking for by taking another simple quiz. Think of the characteristics of that job. What kind of requirements does it have? Would you be making many contacts? Initiating action? Taking risks? Or would the position be such that you couldn't accept risks? Must perform without error? Serve others? Pay attention to detail?

In Figure 5.2 is a *position concept* quiz. The quiz has 24 different job factors that have varying degrees of importance on a job. For each factor, decide its importance and rate it numerically. If the factor has a very low importance, rate it a 1. Give it a 2 if it's low, a 3 if the job has an average requirement for that factor, a 4 if the requirement is high. And score a 5 only for those factors for which

Figure 5.1. Careers Matching Communication Styles

D | **I**

High D, High I

Executive
Manager
Production Planner
Business Developer
Controller
Corporation Lawyer

High I, High D

Sales Engineer
Salesperson "Tangibles"
Labor Negotiator
Management Consultant
Salesperson "Intangibles"
Account Executive

High D, High C

Credit Person
Audio-Visual Producer
Engineer
Inventor—Product Developer
Scientist
Author

High I, High C

Contact Person
Public Administrator
Recruiter
Fund Raiser
Community Recreation Director
Personnel Director

C | **S**

High C, High D

Actor
Commercial Artist
Architect
Chemist
Data Interpreter
Tool Designer

High S, High I

Psychologist
Underwriter
Investment Counsellor
Methods Analyst
Claims Adjustor
Market Analyst

High C, High S

Detailer—Draftsperson
Automation Programmer
Statistician
Actuary
Quality Control Coordinator
Mathematician

High S, High C

Arbitrator
Trust Officer
Survey Analyst
Accountant
Skilled Specialist
Editor

the job has a very high requirement.

Caution: No job requires a 5 on every factor, nor will there be many jobs that have only a 1 requirement for very many. Most of your judgments should be in the 2, 3 or 4 category.

By now you may have guessed that each factor represented one of the behaviors. For example: The first factor, *accepting challenge*, is

Figure 5.2

Position Concept

JOB TITLE: _____

EXAMINED BY: _____

DATE: _____

INSTRUCTIONS

Examine the "job" factors listed below and their relative importance to the job being examined. Using the scale below, give each factor a numerical rating.

1 - Very Low	3 - Average
2 - Low	4 - High
	5 - Very High

THIS JOB REQUIRES THAT I, (he, she):

	ACCEPT CHALLENGE		PERSUADE AND MOTIVATE OTHERS
	WORK MORE WITH PEOPLE THAN THINGS		BE CONTENT WITH REPETITIVE WORK
	MAKE MANY CONTACTS		WORK PRIMARILY IN ONE PLACE
	ACT WITHOUT PRECEDENT		OVERCOME RESISTANCE
	VERBALIZE FLUENTLY		BE GENUINELY OPTIMISTIC AND ENTHUSIASTIC
	INITIATE ACTION		PAY ATTENTION TO DETAIL
	BE RESPONSIBLE FOR QUALITY AND ACCURACY		SERVE OTHERS
	TAKE RISKS		AVOID UNNECESSARY RISK OR TROUBLE
	MAKE A FAVORABLE FIRST IMPRESSION		DRIVE FOR TANGIBLE RESULTS
	EXERCISE SELF-CONTROL		PERFORM WITHOUT ERROR
	COMPLY WITH INSTRUCTIONS		BE A SUPPORTIVE TEAM PLAYER
	BE CAUTIOUS IN MAKING COMMITMENTS		ACCEPT THINGS THE WAY THEY ARE

a High D characteristic. A score of 5 on that factor would indicate you're looking for a position that's High D at least on that one characteristic. A rating of one would show a Low D requirement.

Six of the factors are High D requirements, 6 High I, 6 High S and 6 High C requirements. Turn now to figure 5.3 for a listing of each factor's style identification. Write the factor identifying letter beside each of your responses in Figure 5.2.

Next, add all of your D scores. (You should have 6 responses, and your total should be somewhere between 6 and 30.) Write the total in the box at the top of figure 5.3 after the word *Dominance*. Repeat your scoring for the I factors and write them after the word *Influence*; then continue for the S factors (*Steadiness*) and the C factors (*Compliance*).

Changing these raw scores to percentiles takes a bit of doing. Pay attention now!

Add the totals of your four scores. You'll probably have a sum that's somewhere between 70 and 100 (it'll be different for almost every position). Divide your sum by 4 to get your average score. Write the average in each box under the average heading.[1]

Next, subtract your average score from the total for a characteristic. For example: If your dominance score was 22 and your average score was 19.5, the difference is $+2.5$. To check: Add the differences together. You'll get a plus or minus 1 if you had a remainder you discarded; you'll have a zero if you had no remainders.

Now multiply each difference times 5. To continue with the example above, the D score would now be $+2.5 \times 5 = +12.5$ and the C score would be $-1.5 \times 5 = -7.5$.

Then, add 50 to these scores to get the percentile ranking. For the D score, you'd add $+12.5 + 50 = 62.5$. The C score would be $-7.5 + 50 = 42.5$.

Finally, transfer these percentile scores onto the respective D, I, S, C positions on the graph, and connect the scores with lines to form the profile of the position. This profile can be read for the position much in the same way that your personal communication profile can be read.

Look for the job factors that are high (well above the 50th percentile) and for those characteristics that are low (well below the

---

1. If you have a remainder on the average, drop it if you have 1 left over. If the remainder is a 2, retain it as .5 in the rest of the calculations. If the remainder is a 3, round up your average to the next higher number.

Figure 5.3.   Position Concept Scoring Grid and Profile

Position Concept

	TOTAL	AVERAGE	DIFFERENCE	MUTLIPLE	PERCENTAGE

TOT – AVG · DIF X 5 · 50 - %

JOB TITLE: _____

EXAMINED BY: _____

DATE: _____

DOMINANCE					
INFLUENCE					
STEADINESS					
COMPLIANCE					

PC
D   I   S   C
99
95
90
84
80
70
60
50
40
30
20
16
10
5
1

THIS JOB REQUIRES THAT I, (he, she):

D	ACCEPT CHALLENGE	I	PERSUADE AND MOTIVATE OTHERS
I	WORK MORE WITH PEOPLE THAN THINGS	S	BE CONTENT WITH REPETITIVE WORK
I	MAKE MANY CONTACTS	S	WORK PRIMARILY IN ONE PLACE
D	ACT WITHOUT PRECEDENT	D	OVERCOME RESISTANCE
I	VERBALIZE FLUENTLY	I	BE GENUINELY OPTIMISTIC AND ENTHUSIASTIC
D	INITIATE ACTION	C	PAY ATTENTION TO DETAIL
C	BE RESPONSIBLE FOR QUALITY AND ACCURACY	S	SERVE OTHERS
D	TAKE RISKS	C	AVOID UNNECESSARY RISK OR TROUBLE
I	MAKE A FAVORABLE FIRST IMPRESSION	D	DRIVE FOR TANGIBLE RESULTS
S	EXERCISE SELF CONTROL	C	PERFORM WITHOUT ERROR
C	COMPLY WITH INSTRUCTIONS	S	BE A SUPPORTIVE TEAM PLAYER
C	BE CAUTIOUS IN MAKING COMMITMENTS	S	ACCEPT THINGS THE WAY THEY ARE

50th percentile). Usually, you'll have ranked one or two factors high and the others midrange or low. Then, read off the job characteristics which follow for the one or two factors you've marked as high requirements for the job, and repeat for the factors you've marked as being low requirements. This will give you a word picture of the position you're looking for and its demands.

High D positions demand:

1) Getting results
2) Accepting challenges
3) Making decisions
4) Expediting action
5) Reducing costs
6) Solving problems

Low D positions demand:

1) A protected environment
2) Direction
3) Exercising caution
4) Working predictably
5) Deliberating before deciding
6) Weighing pros and cons

High I positions demand:

1) Contacting people
2) Motivating others
3) Helping people
4) Exhibiting poise
5) Generating enthusiasm
6) Speaking well

Low I positions demand:

1) Concentration
2) Sincerity
3) Reflection
4) Working alone
5) Preference for "things"
6) Thinking logically

High S positions demand:

1) Performing to standards
2) Exhibiting patience
3) Developing special skills
4) Concentration
5) Staying in one place
6) Loyalty

Low S positions demand:

1) Keeping many projects going
2) Seeking variety
3) Dissatisfaction with status-quo
4) Reacting quickly to change
5) Applying pressure
6) Being flexible

High C positions demand:

1) Following directions
2) Concentrating on details
3) Being diplomatic
4) Adhering to procedures
5) Avoiding trouble
6) Controlling quality

Low C positions demand:

1) Assuming authority
2) Acting independently
3) Facing up to problems
4) Stating unpopular positions
5) Delegating
6) Acting without precedent

Generally speaking, the D scale measures authority. If the position is rated high on the D scale, you'll have a lot of authority. The higher the score, the more the authority. And conversely, the lower the D score, the less the authority.

The I score measures the requirement to work with and influence people. A high I score indicates the need to be outgoing and to persuade others to do what you want them to. A low I score indicates that the job is more concerned with things than with people.

The S score can reflect the time requirements of the job. If the score is high on the S, the job doesn't have a great deal of time pressure, and the person in the job doesn't have to move quickly on decisions. If the S score is very low, though, the job may have a great deal of pressure and require that decisions be made quickly and actions taken immediately.

The C score generally measures two things: first, the requirement for attention to detail and accuracy; and second, the degree of independence the position has. A High C requirement indicates that the position requires extreme accuracy and gives almost no independence. The person in the position must follow policy and procedures, and work from precedents. A low C score, on the other hand, indicates that the person in the position would most likely have a great deal of independence of action.

Scores around the midpoint indicate that the position requires an average amount of that type of communication behavior. For D, this would mean the person has an average amount of authority, but must go to someone else for big decisions. For I, the person is expected to be moderately outgoing and able to work with people. The middle score on the S factors means that the person fulfilling the position is expected to be supportive and must have a moderate concern for time. A midscore on the C means some attention to detail and accuracy and some independence.

Making Adaptations in Style to Match Job Requirements

The profile of the position you want and the profile of your personal style may be similar. In this case, you match closely the requirements of the position and should have little difficulty understanding how to communicate on the job.

On the other hand, the profiles may be quite different. Does this mean that you can't perform the job? No. But you do want to look carefully at those differences. Does your ideal job require that you be a High D—and you're a low D? That can be tough. But—you would only have to act like a High D once in a while.

It boils down to this: If a job requires a certain style of performance, it doesn't require it all the time, only situationally. You don't want to place undue stress on yourself by trying to maintain that style constantly. Instead, identify the times when that style is required and sustain it only long enough to get done what has to be done.

How Far Should You Step?

At this point in your life, the degree of risk you're willing to accept is different from that of your youth. Positions are available for people who relish the challenge of a "turnaround" or "startup" situation. If you know you would find these exhilarating and fun, then look for work in these kinds of firms. They will have openings in almost all work areas. But for your own future security, you should investigate completely the circumstances, that is, financing, the personalities and likelihood of replacement for the top management personnel (and your future bosses), the degree of both autonomy and support you would have, the marketability of the company's products or services, pensions and other benefits, and so on.

Your evaluation of the firm's potential would have to include best case, worst case, and mid-range possibilities. Could you survive, fiscally and emotionally, the worst case scenario? (In such high-risk situations, should you fail, the reason will more likely be circumstances over which you have no control rather than any shortcomings on your part.) If your answer is "no," then *don't do it!*

Should You Go into Business for Yourself?

Another high-risk situation that is being taken by more and more older executives is going into business for themselves. One option is to become a consultant to other businesses and business executives. Recently, so many former managers have decided this was a sensible option that in some offices, when you introduce yourself as a "consultant," they respond with, "Oh, so you're unemployed." Cynicism aside, the market for consultants does exist, but only for those older executives who are truly skilled and have specialties for companies which would not hire full-time, in-house specialists. To make consultancy work, you must:

1. Have marketable skills.
2. Know how and be able to sell yourself and your services.
3. Have enough financial reserves to get through the tough beginning stage.
4. Produce the results your client desires when you do sell your services.

Consultancy can be a feast or famine proposition. Even long-established consultants with excellent reputations had difficulty selling their services in the recent recession. Since they were not on a client's payroll, their services were the first to go. They lost promised business, clients canceled contracts outright or renegotiated them for lesser amounts. Consultants who had produced respectable earnings for many years found themselves forced back on the job market as a survival measure.

Still, consultancy—if you are emotionally constituted for the financial ups and downs—can be challenging, exciting and rewarding. Check out the opportunities thoroughly, though, before choosing this as your full-time profession. Talk to other people who are trying to make a living as consultants. Contact consulting groups and ask to talk to one of the consultants about the problems associated with their work. Other possibilities may suddenly be more attractive to you.

Let's say that when you reviewed the things which gave you the most pleasure in life, your woodworking hobby (or some other hobby) was high on the list. Do your hobbies or favorite pastimes have a business in there somewhere? Surprising numbers of former executives are making very good livings out of the things they most like doing.

Were you a successful sales representative for a major firm? How about becoming a manufacturer's representative for several small manufacturers making compatible lines? If you choose high-quality offerings targeted for the markets with which you are already familiar, you could be off and running in a short period of time—and end up with far greater financial rewards with little in the way of up-front expenditures. This is one of the fastest-growing segments in the sales area. Currently, many small manufacturing and importing firms are finding that they have larger sales at less cost handling their sales through manufacturer's reps rather than through on-staff salespeople. The firms can pay higher commissions to their representatives because they're not stuck with the fixed costs of benefits, payroll for nonproducing sales staff, etc. But the risk is, of course, greater for you. You have no benefits, other than those you provide yourself. And you have to pay all of the selling costs—there are no nice company expense accounts, company cars or travel and entertainment allowances.

Other possible career switches to think about: Do you understand personal computers and can you teach? In today's rapidly changing world, the personal microcomputer will be in the homes and offices of a good portion of the population. The computer industry estimates that more than 26 million untrained adults (executives, professionals and hobbyists) will own computers by 1986, with as many as one third of U. S. households and nearly 100 percent of businesses having small computers by 1990. Schoolchildren are being taught how to operate these instruments. But their mothers and fathers need to have someone show them at least the basics. Community colleges, night schools, computer stores as well as a number of new organizations are developing and giving computer instruction. You may not find a full-time job in this, but you may be able to do enough training at night to keep your job search in some other area alive.

What about a totally different second career, one for which you may have to do additional study and preparation? If you're still not sure after going through all of the self-study and introspection suggested so far—it's time to contact a professional. Take the battery of interest, aptitude and skill tests a professional can provide, then make your choice and set your path. Whatever you do, make a considered, rational change—not just one because you're sick to death of your life the way it is. You might not like your new life and career, either.

What about Legal Action to Get Back Your Old Job?

A few years ago, contemplating legal action to regain your job would have been ridiculous. Companies and bosses had almost complete freedom to fire at will, regardless of cause. But recent court cases have made this a whole new ball game.[1] Especially if you were with your company more than 20 years and are at least 55 years old—unless you were caught "stealing, coming in late or drunk, or raping the boss's wife,"[2] then your chances to win a suit against your company are good. Sometimes, just threatening such a suit, especially if all of your personnel evaluations were positive, might be enough to get reinstated. Age cases are currently the fastest-growing segment of discrimination litigation, and are quite frequently being decided in the plaintiff's favor.

If you still retain a copy of your company's personnel handbook, you may want to check to see what it says about employment and about terminations. It may have been written in such a way that it implies an employment contract (although many companies have recently rewritten theirs because of the rash of wrongful firing suits). So, if you feel strongly about your situation, at least discuss it with a lawyer to determine whether you might have grounds for a suit or not.

The federal law, Age Discrimination in Employment Act (ADEA), covers both working people and those seeking employment who are age 40 to 70. A brief summary of its coverage:

> It protects you from discrimination in hiring, in holding on to a job, in wages and salaries, and in fringe benefits and perquisites.

---

1. Major business periodicals and business writers have written at length about this. For example: *Forbes*, August 29, 1983, Sylvia Porter in her June 29, 1983 column; Deborah Watarz and Peter M. Panken in the June 19, 1983, *National Business Employment Weekly*.
2. Kalvin Grove, a partner in the labor law firm of Fox & Grove, quoted in *Forbes*, August 29, 1983, p. 122.

It prohibits advertising which excludes women and older workers.

It doesn't protect you if you've reached the stage where age is a bonafide condition for employment, usually because of public safety (firefighters, police, air traffic controllers, airline pilots).

It doesn't prevent employers from offering incentives for early retirement. But it does prevent them from forcing you to retire against your will. However, they can observe the terms of a seniority system so long as it isn't used to evade the purpose of the ADEA.

It applies to organizations that employ more than 20 workers. (Currently, about 70 percent of all workers are covered by ADEA.)

It permits the mandatory retirement of executives and policy makers at age 65.

If you are disabled, an employer can't force you to retire before age 70 so long as you are able to do the work.

Is it worth it to sue? If you win, yes. The company will have to pay back wages, reinstate you, pay your legal fees, and otherwise settle. If they win, however (and at least the major companies are carefully considering every discharge of an older worker to determine if their position will stand up in court), you will still be unemployed and have a big legal fee to pay.

There are groups and agencies who can help you determine whether you might have a legitimate case or not. These are the same organizations that help older people who are discriminated against in hiring. (See Chapter 11, pages 221-223.) Talking to them before you see your lawyer might save you a bundle.

Ultimately, you'll have to answer the major questions—what kind of job to look for, whether to change careers or not, where to look for a new position, whether to try to regain your old job or not—yourself. If you've considered your ego ideal, determined the communications profile of the job you're looking for and compared it with your own profile, and investigated your answers to some of the other questions raised in this chapter, you should at least be ready to make some of these basic determinations now. And, you'll be able to engage in a more focused and productive job search.

Part 3

The Skills
You Need to
Get that Job

Finding Out
Where the Jobs Are

How long has it been since you looked for a job yourself? Twenty or 30 years? When you first got out of college? If you changed jobs before, the chances are that the job came looking for you, it was a great opportunity and you were actively recruited. Also, as an older executive, you probably met with lots of job seekers over the years. You may be sure that you know the ropes. But—and it's a big but—the shoe's on the other foot now. *You're* the one who's seeking work.

Looking for a job is a marketing problem. And you market yourself through resumés, letters, telephone calls and interviews. But to find out where to look for employment opportunities that match your qualifications, you have to be a detective as well as a marketer. It's true that many of these opportunities will never be listed in the want-ads or at recruitment agencies. You know the reason. The positions aren't open long enough for a public listing. They're filled by internal promotion, by people recommended by company personnel. And they're filled by applicants who keep their "ears to the keyhole," taking advantage of networking to make contacts and get their applications and resumés in before positions are even posted.

As you're aware, jobs are located in two places: the visible market (positions already open and showing in advertisements and personnel office postings) and the invisible or hidden market (jobs not open but that will be opening soon because someone's retiring or leaving, the organization is expanding or new positions are being created). Or the position hasn't even been considered yet. You may have an opportunity to plant the idea for the position in some executive's mind.

What percentage of jobs are filled from each market? According to some experts, the invisible market handles about 75 percent of all available jobs, with 25 percent of the jobs coming from the visible market. Others say the ratio is closer to 80:20 in favor of the hidden market. And in a late 1984 survey of more than 350 major companies, the heads of personnel said they recruited more than a third of their new employees through the visible market. Take your pick of the figures. They still mean that you're going to have to try both markets.

You approach the invisible market differently from the way you would if you were going for a job in the visible market. You're probably aware of most of these ways already, but a little review won't hurt. This many years after the fact, you may have forgotten some of this stuff. And, some of the sources are new and you may not know they're available.

Finding a Job in the Invisible Market

The suggestions in Chapter 3 for learning how to begin your job search are valid ones for approaching the hidden market. The best way to locate a hidden job is through networking—the referral of a friend or business acquaintance. In fact, companies trust the recommendations of their employees so much that some pay a bonus to an employee who recommends someone who's hired and remains working at the firm for a stated period of time (say six months). As an older executive, you probably have more opportunities for this kind of referral than would a younger job seeker. This method is most fruitful when you're looking for the same kind of position in the same business or industry you've worked in before.

But you can approach the hidden market in other ways. None of them is easy, and all require that you expend effort and energy.

Researching Jobs

Let's say that you finished your personal analysis. The results proved to you that you should change industries and/or relocate. Where could you locate the names, addresses, telephone numbers and other information on possible employers? The following sources have provided profitable leads for other job searchers:

Sources of Employer Information

- *College and City Libraries*. Ask for the collections on employment opportunities. Included will be books on job hunting, directories of all kinds, information sources on (including clipping files) local and national businesses. One other resource that shouldn't be overlooked—knowledgeable librarians who know how to locate the information you need and who are usually willing to help.
- *Chambers of Commerce*. These were mentioned earlier as a possible source of help with their job-search courses. The various Chambers also have full information on local businesses, including the general size of the businesses, their addresses, the names of local corporation officers and owners, and often, they may even know about specific hiring needs and opportunities.
- *Better Business Bureau*. To check the trustworthiness of an organization you're interested in, contact the Better Business Bureau of the area where the organization is located. It will provide you with the results of any investigations it's made. The reports are cautiously written, but might prevent you from making a mistake.
- *Fortune* and *Forbes 500*. Once a year, *Fortune* and *Forbes* complete a nationwide survey of all major corporations doing business in the U.S. Each firm is ranked by size, primarily on the basis of the past year's business. Also included are the firms' asset bases, profits, increase or decrease in business compared with the preceding year, the major officers and their incomes plus other information that might be of interest to investors. This information is more up-to-date than the information contained in some of the directories.
- *Value Line Investment Survey*. Provides current up-to-the-minute information on the securities of specific companies.

Primarily a source of "insider" investment information, it still provides good background information on companies looking for turnaround specialists, growth specialists or other management help. Your stockbroker will have copies that you might be able to look at, and libraries with large business collections frequently subscribe to the service.

□ *Trade and Industry Associations.* Begin with the associations you already belong to and those for your industry. Get copies of their publications. Open positions are often announced in the help-wanted ads at the back of the journal. Or you can sometimes get leads on openings by looking in the promotions column.

□ *Federal Job Information Centers.* State capitals and major cities have federal job information centers where openings for federal jobs are posted. In addition, since even many high-level positions require that you take a civil service examination, you can obtain information about taking the test.

□ *Annual Reports.* Some libraries keep these on file as do stockbrokers and financial planning groups. You can also write to companies you're interested in and ask for copies.

Using Directories to Get Information

A good place to begin looking is the Klein's *Guide to American Directories*, which gives information on the different kinds of published directories and the *Encyclopedia of Associations*, which lists the major incorporated national-level (and some state-level) business, trade and nonprofit associations along with addresses and the names of officers.

The *Encyclopedia of Business Information Sources* includes a wide variety of useful information. Because it's an encyclopedia, it does divide information by industry and type of business.

Standard and Poor's Register of Corporations and of *Directors and Executives* is published every year. Employers are listed alphabetically, numerically (by CIS code), and geographically. The listing for each includes brief information about the corporation, its chief business, telephone number, number of employees, names of board members and major executives. The listings in *Standard and*

Poor's Register are very large incorporated businesses. For that reason, very large private businesses are not listed, nor are smaller corporations who don't meet the size requirements of the register. The headquarters address may be the only one given, and the locations of the individual executives are generally not noted. However, for major corporations, it's a fine source of relatively current information. Standard and Poor's also publishes other listings (for example, *Standard & Poor's Stock Reports*), but these are less widely available.

Moody's Industrial Manual lists large industrial (manufacturing) companies whose securities are traded. Employers are listed alphabetically, along with a description of their location, line of business, size and officers. If you're interested in a position in the industrial sector, this book would be a better source for you than *Standard and Poor's Register*.

Moody's Public Utility Manual, Moody's Transportation Manual, Moody's Bank and Finance Manual, and *Moody's Municipal and Government Manual* contain information for other sectors similar to that in *Moody's Industrial Manual*.

The *Thomas Register of American Manufacturers* provides about the same information that's in *Moody's Industrial Manual*, except that in its 12 volumes, it covers nearly every product and product line and nearly all U.S. companies engaged in manufacturing, not just those traded on the stock exchange. Either will be of value to you, and you might want to consult both.

Dun and Bradstreet's Million Dollar Directory and *Middle Market Directory* provide information on smaller companies. Employers are listed alphabetically, numerically, geographically and by product classification. Indicated are the employer's location, telephone number, line of business, sales, total employment and the names of executives.

Fortune's Plant and Product Directory will give you national information on who makes what and where if your experience and interest is with a specific product or product line.

A number of states publish directories on the businesses they've licensed for operation. For instance, the *New Jersey Industrial Directory* lists by county the businesses and industries doing more than a million dollars worth of business. Information includes business location, name of officer in charge, headquarters office address and top executive, number of employees at the site, preceding year's sales, and general type of service or products.

Other useful directories and sources of job information:

State and local

Chamber of Commerce Business Directory
Human Resources Directory (put out by some cities)
Industrial Development Guide
Job Bank books are published in numerous cities and areas. Examples:
  The Boston Job Bank
  The Greater Chicago Job Bank
  The Southwest Job Bank
Membership rosters for various trade and manufacturing organizations
State Education Directory (published yearly or every other year), these list school districts and schools, members of the Board of Education, the superintendent of schools and various supervisory personnel.

National

Ayer Directory of Publications
Directory of National Voluntary Organizations
Federal Jobs
Foundation Directory
Occupational Outlook Handbook
Occupational Outlook Quarterly
Polk's World Bank Directory
Research Centers Directory
The National Job Finding Guides
The Standard Directory of Advertisers
Training and Development Organizations Directory
Women's Organizations and Leaders Directory

Using the Telephone.

The telephone is an excellent tool for contacting the invisible market. Telephone the people referred to you during your networking activities and ask for an opportunity to speak with them in person. Use the telephone as part of a two-pronged search activity—write a letter first to the people and companies identified during research, then follow-up with a telephone call asking for an interview. Of course, the telephone is useful in the visible job market, too. Call company personnel offices to ask if they have job openings in your specialty. Ask to be interviewed for positions advertised in the newspaper. Call employment agencies and recruiters.

Many job hunters don't use the telephone effectively during their job search. Why? Because they're afraid of a turndown. This is the same kind of fear which keeps salespeople from making "cold calls." But judicious use of the telephone can save you hours of driving and walking. And, you can make more contacts in a shorter time than you could otherwise.

Cut down on your anxiety by writing a script to use in making your calls. This is what enables telemarketers to make hundreds of cold calls each day. (It also enables them to talk to the people they want to talk to—and to sell them what they want to sell them!)

Begin by planning the points you want to make. Then write the beginning—the introduction in which you tell why you're calling. After that, explain a little about your background, make the points you want to make, then finish by writing the conclusion of the call (usually a request for an interview or for information of some kind).

Here's the way you might write a script as a follow-up to a letter campaign:

Purpose	**Your Script**
Why you're calling	Hello, this is Betty Graves. You may recall that I sent a letter and a resumé last week in which I explained that I'm looking for a position as a computer analyst with management responsibilities.

Your background	The past five years, I've been working as a computer analyst with the General Electric plastics division. I've been a team leader on a group which completely integrated our manufacturing, inventory management, ordering and invoicing systems. This experience gave me a strong experience in my field. I also have an MBA from Syracuse University.
Why you're looking	Now I want to broaden my responsibilities. I'm looking for the names of firms that might be able to use my skills.
	You may recall some of my strengths: (list one or two of the best ones).
Accomplishments	I'm wondering if you know of any situations in which an organization:
Additional cues	1. Has growing pains and needs an experienced analyst to determine its computer needs and develop or purchase cost-effective programming.
	2. Plans to update existing computer systems and programs.
	3. Wants to develop programs that will integrate the information bases of related departments and activities.
	4. Has an existing computer department and wants to update it to a management information system.
Final cues	Do you have an awareness of any of these situations you'd be willing to share with me?

You might write a similar, but less formal script when you've been referred to someone by a friend or acquaintance. That kind of script might go like this:

Introduction

Hello, my name is Al Mains. David Fast from Pfizer Chemicals suggested that I call you.

(Brief explanation of how you know David.)

Purpose

I'm currently looking for a position as a product manager. I'm looking in the chemical, drug or allied fields. David felt that you were knowledgeable about the job openings in this area and might be able to give me some pointers on whom to see and how I might market myself better to what's available.

(Brief chitchat)

Aim of conversation

I hope we can get together and talk. I'd like for you to check my job campaign so far, and see what suggestions you could make. I can come at whatever time is convenient for you. (Set date and time.)

or

I'm sorry you won't be able to see me. Can you suggest someone else who's knowledgeable about the industry and who might be willing to offer some advice?

A good telephone/letter campaign can get interviews, as can using your networking contacts for referrals. In the beginning, you'll be referring to your script. But as you continue, you'll find that you'll be more comfortable and won't need the script as a crutch. You'll also find that you'll get more tangible leads as you follow through on referrals, and some of them will be for interviews for the hidden jobs you've uncovered.

The best time to call? Between 9:00 and 11:00 A.M. on Tuesday through Friday. If you're calling personnel departments, Friday morning is particularly good, since people don't make too many hiring decisions on Friday. But Monday morning is bad, and Friday afternoon is even worse. That's the time the personnel department conducts its exit interviews for departing employees (and you don't want any part of that activity).

Approaching Jobs in the Visible Market

Don't ignore the "unhidden" market. Thousands of managers and professional people get jobs in this market. They locate their jobs through the classified ads, listings with recruitment firms, placement agencies, corporate personnel departments, civil service offices—and even the state employment services.

Prospecting

Prospecting in the visible market is a little easier than in the hidden market. The resources you'll use are more accessible. You'll need the newspaper, lots of stationery and postage, the telephone directory, good soles on your shoes and persistence.

Personnel offices. Personnel departments are now involved in hiring all but the very top executives in major companies. Telephone calls and visits to personnel offices of companies you'd like to work for could be productive. And conceivably, you might get the jump on a new position by your persistence. Jobs are often requisitioned several weeks or even months before they open. Then they're announced internally for two or three weeks before being advertised in the newspaper. You visit an office, complete an application and ask for an interview. Because the interviewer is aware that the job opening is going to be available, you're interviewed for a position that's essentially still "hidden." Personnel people from different companies also talk to each other and might give you leads on jobs they know are available in another company.

Answering Newspaper Advertisements. Newspaper ads are not always valid job leads. Some advertisers put ads in the paper because they have someone they're unhappy with, and want to shake the trees to see what they can find. But the majority of the ads are for legitimate jobs. And, you shouldn't ignore them as a source of leads.

Some organizations spend big bucks on display ads in the business section of the newspaper; others put little bitty one-inch ads in the classifieds. Regardless of the way they look, ads come in five different forms:

1. The ones that are completely unintelligible. You read the ad and you still don't have any idea what it's for. But if it has the job title that you're looking for, it's worth a telephone call to find out what job they're really advertising.

2. Ads that are intentionally misleading. These are often for the so-called "glamour" industries; for positions that sound as though they are high-level management, marketing or personnel positions; or they may be designed for the greatest possible response. Sometimes, the ads are misleading because the interviewer who wrote the ad didn't realize the ad was ambiguous—or may have had a hidden agenda. You may never get a response to your letter and resumé, but you should still take a chance and send them. You have no way of telling by reading the ad that it's one of this kind.

3. Ads that don't say enough. They don't list essential duties or they use current buzz words as a substitute for substance. You have to study these ads carefully, and sort of "read between the lines" to see what the ad is really about. The ad may have a theme. Use it in your response.

4. Ads that say exactly what they mean. They include job duties and responsibilities and list the minimum requirements for hiring. They may include enough information about the hiring organization that you would know whether or not you'd be interested. To even get an interview on this kind of ad, you'd have to meet or exceed every criteria. But these employers know what they want, and their jobs are worth pursuing.

5. Ads that don't say who the employer will be. These ads may or may not describe the job accurately. But they definitely don't describe themselves. You are asked to respond to initials, to a blind box address at the newspaper, to a box number or a street address. Why don't these employers identify themselves? They may be looking to replace an employee but don't want to signal their intention in advance; they may be breaking the equal opportunity act; they may have marginal jobs, but want them to sound big; or they may simply want to get the resumés without having to respond to the ones that don't interest them.

Other sources of employment ads: trade and association journals.

Agencies and Employment Services

Contacting agencies and employment services for assistance can be thought of as somewhere intermediate between the invisible and visible market. Employment services really run intelligence agencies. They seek information about existing jobs and try to locate people who fulfill the requirements of those positions. Then, they try to get the two together, for a fee.

Executive Recruiters. Employers pay for the services of executive recruiters. They may be retained at a definite fee to work on an exclusive basis to fill a position. Or, they may work on a nonexclusive, contingency fee basis. (They only get paid if they locate someone that can fill the position.) Recruiters are most successful when they work in specific industries or markets. They understand hiring practices and policies and they have rather complete knowledge about the companies who use their services. Executive recruiters often advertise positions that they're trying to fill. But their ads often give only the position title and a salary range. If their ads give more information about the position, they generally disguise their client enough so applicants (or other agencies) can't go directly to the company to apply.

Executive recruiters are good sources to contact. They retain resumés on file if the candidates are well qualified and present themselves well. Since they're working for their clients and not for you, you may not get any action from your visits to executive recruiters. On the other hand, if you fit the needs of one of their clients, they'll work to help you get hired.

Executive recruiters are most frequently located in major cities. You can locate them in the *Yellow Pages* under "Executive Recruiting Consultants," "Management Consultants," "Personnel Consultants," "Employment Agencies," "Technical Search Firms," or some variation of these headings. Some newspapers also have a section that lists recruiters. And you can often get an idea of the agencies that recruit for your field by reading the help-wanted ads.

For additional information about executive recruiters, you can order the *Directory of Executive Recruiters*, published annually by *Consultants News*, Fitzwillia, NH 03447, $15 prepaid. Another source: the membership list of the Association of Executive Search Consultants, 30 Rockefeller Plaza, New York, NY 10012, $4.

Employment Agencies. Until the mid-'70s, most employment agencies charged applicants a fee to get a job. But since then, 80 percent of the agencies have changed to an employer-paid fee. Their ads now say "paid." The primary difference between employment agencies and executive recruiters is in the level of the staff they're recruiting. Employment agencies specialize in clerical, administrative, semiskilled and entry-level positions. However, some employment agencies have more than one division, with one part of the agency recruiting lower-level employees, while another division deals with managerial and professional workers. Some agencies also include temporary placements, managerial and professional as well as clerical. For this reason, if you need temporary work to tide you over, an employment agency might be of help. And temporary work has another advantage. It gives you a chance to get inside a company and look around. And—you just might find a job there.

Management Consultants. Some management consulting firms also do limited executive recruiting. However, they almost never advertise any positions they're looking for, since they're generally on a retainer or the recruiting is being done as a part of a larger project. Management consultants do specialize in certain kinds of businesses and in certain areas of expertise (accounting, computers, planning, etc.). If you know of a consulting firm working in your area of specialization, you might send them a resumé. But, you'll only be asked to come in for an interview if they feel your resumé fits a position for which they're recruiting at that moment.

State Employment Services. When you applied for your unemployment insurance, one of the requirements was that you visit the State Employment Services for an interview and "help." The services seldom have listings for middle- and upper-level managers. But occasionally they'll be knowledgeable about businesses in the area and will provide a good lead. Since you have to go there anyway, you might as well try to get some good out of the experience.

Professional Associations. Some professional associations have placement bureaus as a part of their service to members. If you don't know about the associations to which you belong, write or call to see if they offer this service.

College Placement Services and Alumni Associations. Don't overlook the services your college may be able to give you. Call or write to see if it has a placement service available to older graduates. For teachers and school administrators, for instance, the college services are perhaps the best source of job leads. And jobs for people with professional degrees are also frequently listed.

Other Ways to Look

Outplacement Services. The outplacement specialist is a relative newcomer on the job market. Many of them are hired by companies to help terminated employees look for a job. Essentially, outplacement services are marketing services. They help you learn to market yourself. They'll help you write your resumé (which may be like those of their other clients), write letter campaigns, groom you, give you advice on your search, etc. But they do not get you a job. If you go to an outplacement service on your own, you will get help. But—and it's a big but—you'll pay plenty for it. The charges are often a twelfth to a tenth of your potential salary. And, it's payable in advance, not after you get a job.

Ads in Professional and Trade Publications. Some people have had good luck advertising their availability in newspapers and in professional and trade publications. To be effective, the ads have to be well written, with a selling punch. Newspaper ads seldom draw any responses. Ads in professional and trade publications fare somewhat better. The primary disadvantage is that you can end up spending quite a bit for advertising with no results.

Resumés that Sell

A resumé is not a job getter. You know that. It's a door opener—a sales promotion piece for you. In it, you present information about yourself that will open doors. You include nothing that might keep them closed.

As an older executive you've looked at literally hundreds of resumés over the years. You've used them as screening devices before you interviewed applicants. You can identify almost at a glance the people you'd like to see and those you don't. But did you ever actually analyze the characteristics that the good resumés had that the bad ones didn't? And, how long has it been since you tried to write one? It's lots harder to do this yourself than to evaluate those of others. Also, resumé writing has changed, and you don't want to date yourself by using the same form you used when you were younger.

Why do you need a resumé? Because a well-written resumé is one of your strongest job-hunting tools. It forces you to organize what you've done with your life so that you can give the strongest possible message about your background and experience. It enables you to sell yourself. And, it's a strong "leave-behind" or "go-before" message. It says, "This is what I've done before and can do for you." In short, your resumé is an advertisement about your competence.

It should be easy to understand, dramatically worded and appealing to potential employers. It should present a word picture of your abilities. And it should be concise. It shouldn't try to cover your entire experience and all of your abilities. It doesn't include your negative points or weaknesses.

Potential employers frequently receive hundreds of resumés for positions they have open. (You've probably been faced with a foot-high stack of resumés yourself!) When they're deluged by that kind of response, they look at an individual resumé only seconds. They look to see 1) if the resumé writer has the qualifications, background and experience for the position; 2) if there's anything about the resumé that suggests they should investigate its writer more closely. Then they sort the resumés into piles of "probably interested," "possibly interested" or "not interested." If your resumé lands in "possibly interested" or "not interested" piles, it will never see the light of day again. And, you probably won't hear from the company that they even received your resumé, let alone aren't interested.

When you send letters and resumés as a prospecting device, the screening process is a little different. The person who receives the resumé considers, first, do I have a need for someone with these qualifications, and second, is the person worth spending my time interviewing?

How do potential employers read resumés? The same way you'd read a newspaper story or a lightweight "blood and guts" novel. You look at the headline or title, the beginning paragraph or paragraphs. If this seems interesting, you may read the rest of the article or story. If it's not, you don't continue. Resumés are read the same way. The reader looks at the job title, the job objective or summary, then skims briefly over the rest of the resumé to get an overall impression of the applicant. If the impression is a poor one—the resumé isn't well prepared, is poorly typed, has glaring spelling or grammatical errors (and these have a way of jumping off the page and hitting the looker in the eye!), or shows obvious lack of organizational skill—the resumé is not read further. But if the initial impression is good, the reader goes back to the beginning and reads the resumé more carefully. Point one: your resumé must make a strong initial impression.

You can write several kinds of resumés, each of which has a time and place. The main types of resumés:

□ *Accomplishment or achievement resumés.* These are short resumés in which you give only a tantalizing look at your achievements, your work experience, education and the most important of your skills. The accomplishments are not arranged chronologically, but according to importance. An accomplishment resumé is essentially a "broadside," an ad. It should be restricted to one page or at most, two. Accomplishment resumés are most useful as inserts in letters, and with people who exhibit either High D or High I characteristics.

□ *Chronological resumés.* In these resumés, you arrange your jobs in declining order, most recent to most distant. For each position, you summarize the duties and responsibilities (or give a thumbnail job description). Also include: education, honors, professional memberships, some personal information, and either a job objective or a brief summary statement about your strengths. Chronological resumés *must* be sent to executive recruiters, personnel departments and with any ads that detail the minimum requirements for the position. Use them when applying for positions requiring technical skill such as an accountant, physicist, chemist, financial analyst, mathematician, statistician or engineer. Also, give chronological resumés to people you think exhibit High S or High C communications styles. Chronological resumés might also be best if you have a strong record of achievement in a single field.

□ *Functional resumés.* In these, you arrange your experience in terms of the kinds of jobs or functions you performed. For each function, you describe what you actually did, regardless of when you did it. Also include: a listing of employers, education, honors, personal information and a job objective or summary statement about your strengths. Functional resumés are especially valuable for people who've had several kinds of job experiences, although if they're not done carefully, they can give the impression that you're a job jumper. Functional resumés are good for generalists and when you're applying for a position in a small company in which you might have to wear several hats.

□ *Combination chronological achievement resumés.* In these, you list each job you had, giving a short summary of your duties and responsibilities. Under each job summary you list the notable achievements which set apart your performance on that job from what others might have done. Also include: education, honors, professional affiliations and some personal information. The combination resumé can be given to a person with any communication style since it provides information in the right form for every style. However, they're difficult to keep under control in terms of length and can get too long to be effective.

□ *Letter resumés.* These are resumés in a letter form tailored to answer specific needs or to fit the special requirements of a particular job.

Will you need to write all five kinds of resumés? Perhaps. You'll certainly need more than one if you are looking for and would accept more than one kind of job. But the best resumé to begin with is an Achievement Resumé, primarily because it will make you take a hard look at what you really accomplished, and will force you to see that, "Yes, you really did do some valuable work."

Getting Ready to Write

If you did the exercises in the earlier chapters of this book, you're already well grounded on the information about yourself that's essential to writing a good resumé. If you didn't do those exercises, you can begin with the next step, and come out with a good, selling resumé.

Begin by ruling several pieces of 8½ by 14-inch paper into four columns. (See figure 7.1.)

Step 1. List all of the jobs you've had in the first column. Include dates for each, the names of your immediate superior and the location. If you're not sure of the dates, look them up. Employment dates are one of the few legally verifiable bits of information personnel departments can check, so you'd better get them right. Leave plenty of space between each job listing or put each on a separate sheet of paper.

Figure 7.1

Position Held. Company. Job Title. Superior. Dates.	Duties. Responsibilities. Functions	Accomplishments	Results

Step 2. List the duties and responsibilities for each of those positions in the second column. What were your functions? Take as much space as you need so that you can go back and include other duties and responsibilities as you think of them. Write mini-job descriptions in this column. Don't attempt to polish. This is a working document, so jot down the information as you think of it.

Step 3. Describe what you accomplished. How did you solve problems better than somebody else, what were your sales successes, how did you save the company money, what did you do on that job that set you apart from what somebody else might have done? List each accomplishment separately, even though sometimes individual accomplishments were a part of a larger project.

Step 4. List the results for each accomplishment. What did it actually do for your company? Express results in terms of time saved; money saved or earned; product or services sold; or improvement of some kind. Results should be concrete, not abstract. Use numbers, percentages, actual dollars, not vague terms such as "improved company profitability." If you actually did improve company profitability, state how much or what percentage. For each accomplishment you listed in Step 3, you should write a matching result in this step.

Figure 7.2 illustrates how you might put your worksheet together.

Figure 7.2. Resume Worksheet

Position Held, Company

Duties, Responsibilities, Functions

Accomplishments

Results

> managed headquarters accounting staff of 38 people
> installed new computer system which integrated
> purchasing, manufacturing, warehousing,
> inventory control, ordering, billing, accounts

receivable and payable, forecasting, profit-
planning and other aspects of financial control
wrote accounting and audit procedures for the new
computer system
revised other policies and procedures for the accounting department
administered accounting procedures
set company audit policy (none existed)
trained headquarters staff in correct procedures
reorganized the department reporting relationships
developed new reporting procedures
member of corporate planning and acquisitions
committee
lead member of corporate product-pricing and profit-
planning committee
led several study groups on special corporate
assignments
set up accounting and reporting procedures for
branch offices
made at least one visit per year to each branch office
(accounting managers reported to me)
trained 35 branch accounting managers in correct
procedures (the managers were then responsible
for training their own people

UNITED BRANDS, INC.   1966-1985
Boston, MA

Controller   1978-1985

cut down on capital required to finance inventory	freed $1.5 million for use in corporate expansion
reduced time between shipping and customer billing from three days to one	increased cash flow; reduced aged accounts by 12%
shortened response time to customers	cut complaints by 35%
improved forecasting and planning	better financial control
cut staff time required to learn new system	saved estimated $150,000 in running duplicate systems
simplified department activities, reducing time requirements	cut staff from 45 to 38 people
clarified relations with auditors	reduced audit expenses 15%
increased skills of department staff members	reduced error rate to less than 1%; cut input time 15%
established supervisors and lead accountants	freed self to serve on special study groups
cut time to produce EOM reports	from 15 days to 3 days EOM

prepared feasibility study for new plant; study accepted by committee	plant built; costs within 5% of estimates; new plant increased profits 25% in first year of operation
uniform reporting of transactions to headquarters	reduced time to produce consolidated reports by 1/3
developed rapport within company	reduced telephone time spent on problems
improved branch performance	increased staffing at 8 branches, reduced staff at 13
increased sense of responsibility of individual branch managers	

When you've completed this task, on a single page, write down the colleges and universities you attended, in reverse chronological order, by date of attendance. Indicate the degrees you received. If part of your professional competence was learned in short courses, list those, too. (You seldom list these on a resumé, but might want to mention one or more in a cover letter sometime.)

On another page, note membership or affiliation with professional organizations and associations. Include any licenses you may hold. Also note any offices you held.

If you've published or received any honors, list these on another sheet or two of paper. (Some prolific writers may need several pages for this.) If you hold any patents, list those. (You may have to do some real research to organize all of this stuff.)

Don't spend any time on your social or personal life. Most of those items are no longer germane and shouldn't be used in a resumé. However, if you have some specific personal skills that would be of value to an employer, you might want to list those: for instance, languages spoken or officer of a community organization such as the Chamber of Commerce or the United Fund.

You now have the raw material that you'll need to write your resumé. Suggestion: three-hole punch the papers and keep them in a notebook. You'll use these resources to write your stand-alone resumés and cover letters and tailored letter resumés you'll send to potential employers.

What about Age and Dates?

The 1975 Age Discrimination Employment Act did away with the requirement that potential employees give their birthdates and/or ages on job applications. You absolutely *do not* include your age or birthdate on a resumé. You don't include the dates you attended or graduated from high school or college—which also tell your age. Don't even go back to the beginning of your employment career to list every job you ever held. For most older job seekers, showing the last 15 to 20 years of employment is plenty. Those were the years, anyway, when you most likely accomplished the tasks you want to stress on your resumé.

The breadth and depth of your accomplishments, in fact, is one argument against using a functional resumé. Detailing all of the functions you've mastered can reveal your general age because no one could have done that much without living and working quite a while.

General Suggestions for Resumé Writing

The best suggestion you can get from anyone on how to write a resumé is this: write it simply and clearly so that it can't possibly be misunderstood. Use short sentences, short, powerful words, lots of verbs and not many nouns and modifiers.

Resumé "Do's" and "Dont's"

The following Do's and Dont's might be considered to be the Ten Commandments of resumé writing.

1. Use short statements and abbreviated sentence structure. You don't use the words I, you, we, our anywhere. The sentences have no subjects, or have descriptive subjects, i.e., accountant, administrator, manager, communicator. You should be pungent, not poetic; express ideas powerfully, not passively.

2. Use brevity, not verbiage. If one word will tell the important point, use it. Write *directed* rather than *controlled* and *supervised* or *controlled, directed* and *managed*.

3. Include only one thing in each statement. Do not combine unrelated functions, tasks or accomplishments. Keep them separate so that the reader can understand them. Don't mistake economy of words with combining unrelated tasks or

accomplishments. For instance, market research and personal sales are both in the general field of sales. But each should stand alone.

4. Begin each sentence with an action. Start as many sentences as you can with a verb. "Increased sales as a result of market analysis," is much stronger than, "After study, research, investigation and analysis, was able to increase sales."

5. Clarity. Use the word that is most precise and informative. Gear your choice of words to the audience you intend for the resumé. You would write the same achievement in general terms for a marketing audience, a general manager or the personnel department; you would use technically precise words if the resumé was going to a technical manager. But use industry-specific words only if the majority of the people who might receive your resumé would understand them. (If you'll be sending resumés to several kinds of audiences, you might want to write several versions of the same achievement to keep in your file or word processor.) The word choice rule of thumb: the simpler, the better.

6. Avoid gobbledygook. Don't leave it to your reader to guess what you mean or what you intended to say. Don't say that you "coordinated the customer service function" when you actually "cooperated with the customer service manager" in your role as national sales manager. Don't write ambiguous statements or those that might mean several different things.

7. Use appropriate language to the position you're looking for. The words a chief executive would normally use are quite different from those employed by a factory supervisor. Use the language that best expresses your level of authority and scope of responsibility.

8. Narration and reader appeal. In trying for short statements and clarity, don't sacrifice the continuity of the story you're telling. Be dynamic, but not spasmodic. Connect statements and paragraphs to prevent your resumé from being a collection of disjointed statements and paragraphs. The resumé should reflect some kind of theme or unifying principle.

9. Illustrate. Point out specifically what you did, how well you did it and how your employer benefited. Use the illustrations with discretion. Don't overpower your readers with so many examples that they can't understand what you really did and what your

responsibilities were.

10. Sell yourself. In writing a resumé, modesty will get you nowhere.

One of the commandments suggested that you "choose the strongest verbs you can to explain what you did." Show action and power. The following list of verbs do just that. Refer to it when you're looking for the one "right" word.

achieved	bought	coordinated
acquired	broadened	corrected
acted	budgeted	corresponded
activated	built	counseled
adapted		created
addressed	calculated	cultivated
administered	captured	
advertised	catalogued	decentralized
advised	centralized	decreased
advocated	challenged	defined
affected	changed	demonstrated
allocated	clarified	designed
amended	collaborated	determined
analyzed	collated	developed
anticipated	collected	devised
appointed	combined	directed
appraised	communicated	disapproved
approved	compiled	discovered
arranged	composed	disseminated
assembled	conceived	distributed
assessed	concluded	documented
assisted	condensed	doubled
assumed	conducted	drafted
audited	constructed	
augmented	consummated	edited
averted	contacted	effected
avoided	contracted	eliminated
	converted	employed
based	conveyed	enforced

encouraged
engineered
enlarged
established
estimated
evaluated
executed
exercised
exhibited
expanded
expedited
explained
exposed
extracted

facilitated
forecast
formed
formulated
fortified
framed
fulfilled

generated
governed
grouped
guided

handled
helped
hired

identified
implemented
improved
improvised
increased
incurred

informed
initiated
innovated
inspected
inspired
instigated
instituted
instructed
insured
interpreted
interviewed
introduced
invented
investigated
isolated

judged
justified

launched
led
lightened
liquidated
localized
located

maintained
managed
marketed
minimized
moderated
modified
monitored
motivated

negotiated

obtained

operated
organized
originated
oversaw

perceived
performed
pioneered
planned
prepared
presented
presided
prevented
processed
procured
produced
programmed
promoted
proved
provided
published
publicized
purchased

reacted
received
recommended
recorded
recruited
rectified
redesigned
reduced
referred
refined
regulated
rejected
related
renegotiated

reorganized	set up	surveyed
replaced	settled	systemized
reported	shaped	
represented	simplified	taught
researched	singled out	terminated
reshaped	sold	tested
resolved	solved	traded
revamped	sparked	trained
reviewed	specified	transferred
revised	spoke	translated
revitalized	staffed	tripled
routed	standardized	
	stimulated	uncovered
saved	streamlined	undertook
scheduled	strengthened	upgraded
secured	studied	used
selected	submitted	utilized
settled	supervised	
separated	supplied	vitalized
served	supported	
serviced	surpassed	wrote

Words used in ads and in job descriptions are frequently unsuitable for resumés. They may be weak, ambiguous or misleading. The same is true for job titles--Administrative Officer or Management Executive are redundant and don't describe any known job. The title you had in your last job may have that meaning only in your company. For instance, in one company a Customer Service Manager may be part of Marketing, in charge of order processing, complaints, and customer communications; in another company, a Customer Service Manager is in charge of repairs and technical assistance.

So be sure that in addition to job title, you explain what you're looking for and what you did with that title.

Other words may not be effective. Look at the words below. These words are weak, nonspecific, vague or tricky. They don't add much, and may detract from your meaning.

extensive	vague	implies incomplete coverage
considerable	weak	more than a little, but not much
executive	vague	implied random responsibilities
administrative	weak	clerical side of the job
diversified	unspecific	jack of all trades
assisted	weak	in charge of no phase of anything
participated	weak	can't accept much credit
inaugurated	weak	implies only that something got started under you
competent	weak	no great shakes in own opinion
qualified	weak	can, but never had the chance to
assigned to	weak	use "took charge of" instead
handled	vague	can mean almost anything
coordinated	tricky	means whatever you mean it to
general	vague	has no definite meaning

Writing Achievement Statements

Key to selling yourself is to show that you've accomplished, if not miracles, at least solid worthwhile achievements. For each job you had, you've already listed both major and minor accomplishments. (Your chart should be similar to that shown in Figure 7.2.) For each job, check the achievements you think are most marketable for the position(s) you're seeking. Select 12 to 15 of the most important achievements to polish.

The most effective way to present these accomplishments? Using the PAR formula is one way. P = Problem, A = Accomplishment, R = Result. How do you write them? This way. For each accomplishment chosen, ask yourself, "What was the problem I was solving when I accomplished this? What actions did I take? What result did I get and what did it do for my employer?"

For the sake of argument, let's say that you managed a purchasing department. You were very concerned with the efficiency of the department. It took your purchasing agents too long (an average of one week) to issue their purchase orders and that ultimately delayed deliveries. A statement of the problem: you needed to reduce the time between receiving the requisition and issuing the purchase order.

Write down the action you took first. What was it you did? Example: (*Action*) Revised purchasing procedures.

Write what the results were next. Example: (*Action*) Revamped purchasing procedures, (*result*) cutting department costs by 15 percent and the error rate by 5 percent.

Finally, write the problem showing the correction. Example: (*Action*) Revamped purchasing procedures, (*result*) cutting department costs by 15 percent and the error rate by 5 percent, and (*corrected problem*) reducing the average time between receipt of requisition and purchase order issuance from one week to three days.

Note that in this statement, concrete and measureable figures are given. Reduced costs 15 percent, error rate by 5 percent, time from one week to three days.

As you rewrite each statement, continue to ask yourself, what action did I take, what were the results, what did the action change and how much did it change (the problem). Stating the problem does not necessarily mean that something was wrong. In the sense used here, a problem can be due to a specific condition that needs to be corrected or worked around; it can be a situation that needs to be changed or taken advantage of; or it could be an assignment you received and made work for you.

If in correcting a problem, you accomplished several things, you might use a slightly different format to express problem, action, result. In the example, one problem spawned several accomplishments and results.

Example:

Revamped purchasing procedures, which reduced the average time from receipt of requisition to purchase order issuance from one week to three days and resulted in:

□ Reduction of department costs by 15 percent.
□ A 5 percent cut in error rate.
□ An improved system of following-up on orders.
□ A valid way to measure the purchasing effectiveness of individual purchasing agents.

119

The following statements illustrate other ways in which the writers developed acceptable wording for their achievement statements.

---

1. Planned and directed all phases of a company turnaround which:
   - Achieved an 84 percent increase in sales, including the introduction of new product.
   - Eliminated losses of $2.5 million within a three-year period.
   - Reduced selling and administrative expense ratios from 21 percent to 15 percent of sales.

2. Expanded production 17 percent at no cost by restoring previously inoperable equipment and setting up an additional assembly line.

3. Increased market share and doubled product line sales by $5,000,000 the first year by teaching salespeople to sell systems rather than components.

4. Reduced losses of a multicompany real estate developer by:
   - Simplifying accounting procedures to provide rapid cost information. This information led to a decision to close a division.
   - Operating the accounting department with reduced staff, saving $125,000 annually.
   - Accelerating project completion by avoiding expensive litigation.

5. Consulted with a $1 billion + chemical operation of a diversified Fortune 100 company. Proposed and investigated potential acquisitions and successfully urged the strategic redeployment of assets which improved the return by 5 percent.

Writing Statements
Showing Duties, Responsibilities, Functions

In the chronological, functional, combination and letter resumés, you tell the reader about the kind of work that you did—your duties, responsibilities, job functions. But you still keep in mind that you accomplished something doing those things. That doesn't mean that you necessarily use dollars, time, percentages or words that indicate accomplishment. But you do show that your actions did something for the company.

For instance, a *controller* for a major national concern wrote on his worksheet that he:

Managed headquarters account staff of 38 people.

Installed new computer system which integrated
purchasing, manufacturing, warehousing, inventory control, ordering, billing, accounts receivable and payable, forecasting, profit-planning and other aspects of financial control.

Wrote new accounting and audit procedures for the new computer system.

Revised other policies and procedures for the accounting department.

Administered accounting procedures.

Set company audit policy (it was nonexistent).

Trained headquarters staff in correct procedures.

Reorganized the department reporting relationships.

Developed new reporting procedures (that cut time required for production of corporate reports).

Member of corporate planning and acquisitions committee.

Lead several study groups on special corporate assignments.

Set up accounting and reporting procedures for branch offices.

Made at least one visit per year to each branch office (accounting managers reported to me).

Trained 35 branch accounting managers in correct procedures (the managers were then responsible for training their own people).

How can these be condensed and capsulized for the greatest impact? First, analyze the activities for those which have a similar theme. For instance, this controller listed seven different items that were related to policies and procedures. He set policy, wrote it, trained headquarters personnel and branch managers in correct application of the policies and procedures, and administered to see that they were followed.

Three items talk about the staff he managed or had ultimate responsibility for: he managed 38 headquarters staff members, 35 branch managers reported to him (he visited each branch at least once a year), and he reorganized reporting relationships.

Two items related to the installation of a new computer system: one mentioning the functions that were integrated, the other about writing new computer procedures.

He was a member of several corporate standing committees, he led several special project committees.

Figure 7.3 illustrates how he combined these into duties, responsibilities and function statements suitable for a chronological resumé.

Figure 7.3.   Duties, Responsibilities, Function Statements

Installed new computer system, including equipment and programs, integrating for the first time the purchasing, manufacturing, warehousing, inventory control, ordering, billing, accounts receivable and payable, forecasting, profit-planning and financial control functions.

Established company policy on audits and on use of new computer system; revised existing accounting procedures for headquarters and branch offices; trained headquarters staff and branch managers on correct application of policies and procedures; monitored both groups for compliance.

Organized reporting relationships for headquarters and branch accounting groups; directly managed 38 member headquarters accounting staff; responsible for performance of 35 branch accounting groups.

Led study groups on special corporate assignments; voting member (one of five) of corporate product-pricing and profit-planning committees; member of corporate planning and acquisitions committee.

For a combination chronological/achievement resumé, these statements would have to be condensed. He would integrate some of his functions into achievement statements, and highlight them under the "job description."

Job Objectives or Thumbnail Sketches?

Most of the books on resumé writing emphasize the importance of writing good job objectives for your resumés. These are the second item on standard resumés after the name, address and telephone numbers. However, for the older executive or professional, including the term "job objective" or "employment objective" doesn't do justice to that person's status, background and experience.

Instead, head a section with the job title that is being pursued. Under that heading, write a "thumbnail sketch" or word picture that illustrates your strengths and abilities. The sketch could also give some idea of the background, industry or area in which you have already performed. The sketch is more powerful than a job objective. And by describing what you can do, you are essentially describing the kind of job you want. The thumbnail sketch in essence is both a job objective statement and a good advertisement.

How do you write one? First of all, you don't begin writing your resumé by writing your thumbnail sketch. You may choose the job title first, or at least the general area (say Marketing) that you're going to pitch your resumé toward. After you've written the rest of the resumé in a draft form that you think you can live with, write the thumbnail.

Guidelines for Writing the Thumbnail

1. Choose an accurate job title for the position you're pursuing.
2. Each statement in the thumbnail should be tied in to the job

title. It should be some ability or characteristic that would help you do that job better.

3. Keep the thumbnail sketch short (somewhere between 30 and 55 words, with the ideal being around 40). Don't write complete sentences. Use descriptive phrases or telegraphed sentences.

4. Use highly descriptive verbs or nouns to describe what you can do. Use modifiers only when they add to the concrete impression. (Don't use any of the weak modifiers mentioned earlier.)

Remember, you're writing an "ad" when you're preparing the thumbnail. Does what you've written sell? This is a case where you have to sell the sizzle with the steak.

Samples of Thumbnail Sketches

Purchasing Manager. Experience purchasing professional with comprehensive background in organization and administration. Successful record of cost reduction. Expertise in inventory control, subcontracting of production parts, warehousing and transportation. Experienced in EDP application. Certified Purchasing Manager.

Business Systems Analyst. Identifies and solves business problems. Creates time and cost-effective manual and EDP systems. Effective coordinator of human, financial and material resources. Consultant to management, giving advice on the effective use of EDP systems.

Public Relations Executive. Public Education/Information Director. Expert at transforming ideas into successful programs. Skilled recruiter and motivator. Creator of health-improvement programs for diversified clubs, civic organizations, patient and youth groups, and employees. Persuasive public speaker and agency spokesperson.

Advertising/Sales Promotion Executive. Creative developer and producer of marketing-support programs for domestic and international companies. Skilled organizer. Solid company and agency background. Perceptive translator of complex technical data into clear selling concepts.

Senior Engineering Consultant. Strong, innovative, profit-oriented executive. Can lead industrial engineering department in multidiscipline projects involving design of production and product equipment to increase productivity, reliability and efficiency. This includes mechanical, electromechanical, chemical, ultrasonic, hydraulic and pneumatic devices. Personally developed over three dozen original items. Professional engineer, MSIE.

International Sales and Marketing Executive, Industrial Products. Effective organizer and international operations strategist. Highly skilled closer. Knowledgeable in markets and cultures worldwide. Adept at motivating and communicating with sales forces and technical service personnel. Multilingual.

Financial Manager. Profit oriented executive with broad experience in finance and administration. Effective manager of accounting and data-processing departments. Skilled in design and implementation of accounting and management systems. Analytical and creative problem solver. CPA.

Editorial Management. Innovative, practical manager experienced in planning, developing, writing/editing and coordinating books and multimedia materials for publication. Editorial competencies: sales and marketing; general management; arts and crafts "how to books"; and elementary and second language arts, reading, science and social studies. Special skills in devising sales and marketing strategies and training. Platform speaker and presenter.

Other Sections of the Resumé

You can include a number of different sections in your resumé. Several of them are almost mandatory: you should include something on your education and on your business affiliations (achievement resumé). And usually, but not always, you'll include a personal section.

Education. In every resumé, you should include a section on education. Young people are advised to include their dates of attendance or the date they received their degrees. You'll have to give this information when you make a formal application so that the potential employer can check on your credentials. But you don't have to put it on a resumé, and you shouldn't. Unless you earned some spectacular kind of honor in college, say Phi Beta Kappa, simply list the universities and colleges you attended, in reverse order, along with any certificates or degrees. If you've had short courses and seminars, you could list them if they're important to what you currently do. Otherwise, omit them entirely or provide a summary statement.

Example:

Education

University of Illinois	MS in Biochemistry
DePaul University	BS
Belleville Community College	AA

Numerous short courses and seminars on various phases of general management and biochemical laboratory procedures

---

Business Affiliations. This section is included when you write an achievement resumé. It is placed immediately after the education section. In it, you simply list the companies you worked for and your job title. You don't state the dates worked. You can include some identifier, such as "a division of———" when you worked for a subsidiary of a major corporation, and give some idea about the line of business, and its location. But if you're trying to get the resumé on a single page, then the following format (most recent to distant) will suffice:

Business Affiliations

Omni/Penthouse Publications, Ltd.	Director Financial Planning
Schatz Bearing Co., Inc.	Director Finance/Administration
Dutchess County Government	Budget Director/Controller
Savin Corporation	Assistant Controller
RCA Corporation	Cost & Budget Supervisor

Professional Affiliations. For jobs in which professional certification or membership in professional or trade organizations is a must, this heading should be included. Or, you can use a heading called Other Affiliations, and include business and community organization memberships *that show your competence*—for instance, president of the Chamber of Commerce, chairman of fund raising for United Fund.

Example:

Professional Affiliations

New York State Society of Certified Public Accountants
National Association of Accountants

Military Experience. You may choose to include this or not, depending upon your rank and whether or not the experience your military service gave is transferrable to civilian life.

Honors, Publications, Patents. This heading (or it can be more than one heading) shoud be included in any resumé *if it adds to hireability.* If you're listed in any of the *Who's Who* books, it's nice to include it. And published papers and books also add to stature as do patents granted. You use a telegraphed format for these, too. Simply list the names of the articles or books (without publisher), describe the patent in some way (don't give it an esoteric title), briefly identify the honor.

Personal. Most personal questions are no longer the legally valid concern of an employer. You can put a minimum amount of information in this section—or you can leave it out altogether. Prospective employers don't need to know you're married, divorced or single (unless being single is a requirement, as it is in some international work where housing isn't available for married employees). How many children you have is none of their concern, either. You might want to mention that you're active in civic and community affairs, although mentioning that you're active in your religion can be a deselector. And you should include the phrase, "Willing to relocate/travel" or something similar, even if you really don't want a job that will require you to move.

Different Kinds of Resumés

As mentioned at the beginning of the chapter, you'll write different resumés for different purposes. For some of you, the only resumé you'll ever need is either the Chronological or the combination Chronological/Achievement resumé. In fact, if you're only going to write one resumé, the best format is probably the Achievement/Chronological Resumé. However, to write that one correctly, you'd have to first do all of the work it would take to write both an Achievement and a Chronological resumé, so you can't do that just to save time.

Interim or Temporary Resumé

Putting together a good resumé takes time. Give yourself the time you need to do it right. In the interim, put together a temporary resumé to use until the good one is ready. At the top of the page, write your name, then your address and telephone number. List your education next (most recent first), and military service, if you were in the military. Follow that with your business affiliations (most recent first). List the employer you worked for, your job title and brief explanation (a short paragraph) of what you did for that employer. Finally, include a short personal section that mostly says that you'll "travel and relocate." You should be able to get this on less than two sheets of paper.

Achievement Resumé

Now that you know how to write achievement statements, writing an achievement resumé should be a snap. Begin by writing your name, address and telephone numbers. If you don't have an office or an answering service, don't include a business number. And give an alternate number—say that of a friend who's generally available—where the telephone will be answered.

Next, write your job title as a heading, then place your thumbnail sketch, in indented paragraph form, under the heading.

The next heading should read *Selected Achievements*. Under that heading, choose five to eight of the best achievements you have that illustrate the accomplishments you've made in similar jobs. Put the best achievement first, the next best second, the third best last, and spread the others out in between.

Follow the selected achievements with the *Education* section, the *Business Affiliations* section, then any of the other optional sections which you feel should be included. Place the personal section last or omit it altogether.

Figure 7.4 illustrates the way one executive completed his achievement resumé.

Figure 7.4.   Achievement Resume

Ronald M. Benjamin

> 60 Hickory Wood Drive, Ridgewood, IL 60769
> Office: (217) 555-8686   Home (217) 555-9210

GENERAL MANAGER

Successful record of profit improvement, cost reduction and financial control. Skilled in marketing, manufacturing, improving operating results and return on investment. Strong leader, problem solver, communicator and motivator. Demonstrated ability in acquisitions, labor negotiations and strategic planning.

SELECTED ACHIEVEMENTS

Planned and directed all phases of a company turnaround which:

- Achieved an 84% increase in sales, including the introduction of new products; eliminated losses of $2.5 million within a three year period.

- Reduced selling and administrative expenses from 21% to 15% of sales.

Relocated a manufacturing facility, reducing product cost 15% and improving productivity 25%.

Initiated and directed a marketing expansion program, increasing sales by 50% and profits $1.5 million.

Reorganized a $60 million division, reversing a $1.2 million loss to a $2.2 million profit within a two year period.

Directed a corporate-wide energy conservation program which resulted in an annual savings of $275,000.

Negotiated an acquisition and integrated it as an operating division, increasing annual sales by 20% in the first year.

Initiated and directed a multi-plant facility consolidation, discontinuing manufacture of unprofitable products. Increased profits by $700,000 and reduced working capital requirements by $500,000 in the first year.

BUSINESS AFFILIATIONS

Trendeast Industries	President/General Manager
Trendeast Plastics	Executive Vice President
Trendeast Industries	Group Vice President
	Vice President & Controller
	Corporate Budget Director

EDUCATION

University of Illinois	Executive Development Certification
Rider College	B.S. in Accounting

PROFESSIONAL AFFILIATIONS

American Management Association, President's Group
National Association of Accountants
Past Director of Cerebral Palsy Association
Past Director of Ridgewood Chamber of Commerce

PERSONAL

Will travel/relocate

Chronological Resumé

The chronological resumé begins exactly like the achievement resumé. You list your name, address and telephone numbers, then the job title and thumbnail sketch are next.

The next heading can be *Background and Experience, Business Affiliations, Experience, Relevant Experience, Employment History* or *Business Record.* For each position you've held, give your job title, your employer, and some identifier about the employers' business, if you feel it's necessary. Then, write in the duties, responsibilities, functions statements for that position.

The next section should list your education, followed by any of the other sections which you feel would be helpful. You may want to include some narrative in an honors or patents section, and you may increase the amount of information in the business and community organizations and personal section. And you may want to detail your military service a little more. You're writing a chronological resumé for people who are concerned with detail, and you should supply it.

Figure 7.5 gives an example of a chronological resumé.

Figure 7.5. Chronological Resume

William N. Lloyd

315 East 35th Street, Apt. 5D   New York, New York 10017
Home: (212) 555-1015   Office: (212) 555-6900

INTERNATIONAL SALES/MARKETING MANAGER

Effective, aggressive market developer and innovator. Perceptive analyzer of sales markets and situations. Skilled manager of foreign personnel.

EXPERIENCE

GENERAL ELECTRONICS, LTD.

1980-1985: Manager, Apparatus and Component Sales, Athens, Greece

Managed sales efforts in Africa and the Middle East for electronics equipment, systems, packages, repair parts and components used both by military and industrial organizations. Hired and trained salespeople, set up branch offices, negotiated agreements with distributors and manufacturer's representatives who were foreign nationals. Analyzed highly competitive markets, developed sales strategies, made high level contacts with government and industrial groups. Managed Mideast regional office in Athens.

1977-80: Manager, East Mediterranean Sales

Directed sales of electronics equipment to all classes of customers in Cyprus, Greece, Iraq, Jordan, Lebanon, and Syria. Managed branch office in Athens. Developed non-traditional markets by establishing and training a multi-country sales organization, 60% of whom were foreign nationals.

1971-1977: Senior Sales Engineer

Responsible for penetrating new markets and increasing market share in Latin America. Arranged for custom engineered electronics equipment and components. Assisted customers to resolve technical problems.

1964-1971: Product Specialist

Developed new sales territory in Southeastern United States. Exceeded assigned quotas each year.

MARKELL ELECTRONICS

1960-1964: Sales Engineer, Technical Marketing Program

Developed new market segments and increased sales in a territory believed to be at a saturation level; created a new stocking program for distributors.

EDUCATION

Georgia Institute of Technology   M.S.
Virginia Military Institute   B.S.

Numerous short courses and seminars on marketing, sales management, international trade and general management

MILITARY

1st Lieutenant, U.S. Army, Vietnam 1964-66

PROFESSIONAL AFFILIATIONS

American Marketing Association
Sales and Marketing Executives Club of New York

PERSONAL

Will travel/relocate
Speaks Spanish, Italian, Greek and Arabic

Functional Resumé

When the position you're applying for incorporates several different functions, and you've had experience in each, and possibly in other related areas, the functional resumé is called for. You can write the statements you plan to include in the achievement format. Or, you use the duties, responsibilities, functions statements if they're more illustrative of your competencies.

The resumé begins as do the achievement and chronological ones.

Your name, address, telephone number, the job title you're looking for and the thumbnail.

The next heading you'd list as *Selected Achievements, Related Experience* or simply *Experience*. Then, you place subheadings, such as "Management," "Planning," "Manufacturing," and "Technical." After each subheading, you place the achievement or duties, responsibilities, functions statements that are illustrative of the subheading.

The rest of the resumé is completed much as are the other resumés. The education section, a business affiliation section (so the employers you worked for and your job titles are listed), then add any of the other sections you think are needed.

Figure 7.6. Functional Resume

Rowena Jackson
6518 Pinon Drive
Santa Fe, NM 87501
Home: (505) 555-1012
Office: (505) 555-2250

PUBLIC RELATIONS EXECUTIVE

Creative public relations generalist, skilled in handling wide range of promotional assignments and media relations, including university and foundation publicity and fundraising. Versatile writer. Strong editorial and production background. Self-starter. Effective under pressure.

PROFESSIONAL HIGHLIGHTS

UNIVERSITY: **Associate Director,** Brigham Young University Fund

Organized and directed public relations program; wrote fundraising brochures, newsletters; prepared correspondence and coordinated communications with classes and alumni; managed special events, media contact.

Associate Director University Relations, Idaho State University

Directed professional editors, writers, photographers and printers who developed publicity, advertising and publications for the University. New advertising campaign and innovative marketing approach expanded student enrollments.

133

PUBLIC RELATIONS COUNSELING FIRMS:
Account Executive, Hill & Knowlton

Supervised publicity and public relations projects for both corporate and non-profit clients. Projects included brochures, annual reports and executive speeches.

COMMUNITY AND HEALTH AGENCIES:
Associate Director of Public Relations, National Multiple Sclerosis Society

Planned and executed media information programs for TV, print and radio. Supervised and edited writing, layout, photography and production for publications; conceived, researched, wrote and/or edited speeches to obtain extensive media coverage.

Director of Public Relations, Santa Fe Opera Company

Prepared publicity and public relations projects and programs for all media during extensive fundraising campaign. Produced a television special, annual reports, newsletters, speeches, feature articles, press releases and brochures.

BROADCAST MEDIA:
Writer/Director/Producer, KISU

Wrote, produced and directed segments on the six o'clock nightly news program.

TEACHING:
Lecturer, Brigham Young University, Idaho State University, University of New Mexico

Taught courses on communications and public relations.

EDUCATION

New York University, School of Education   M.A.
University of California   B.A.

PERSONAL

Will travel/relocate

Combination Chronological/Achievement Resumé

A chronological/achievement resumé is easy to develop if you've already written an achievement and a chronological resumé. The section is called *Selected Experience and Accomplishments.* You can use the materials you've already prepared for the other two resumés. Begin with your name, address and telephone numbers.

Next comes your old friend the job title and thumbnail sketch.

Third is the Selected Experience and Accomplishments. You place the jobs in the same order as on a chronological resumé—most recent to those in the past. List the company, your position, then the description of your duties, responsibilities and/or functions. (From the chronological resumé.) Then indented underneath the job description, arrange three or four accomplishments you achieved working at that position. Place the most important accomplishment first and the second most important one last. Generally speaking, you'll want to include a longer job description and more accomplishments with your most recent positions, decreasing the length of the job description and the number of accomplishments as you go back in time.

The rest of the resumé is completed exactly as any other resumé. Include education and personal headings. (You don't need the business affiliation heading since your employers are included in the selected experience and accomplishments section.) Add any other categories from professional, community or business organizations; honors, awards, patents and publications. Include military service, especially if it was lengthy and you had a relatively high rank.

Figure 7.7 illustrates a combination chronological/achievement resumé.

Figure 7.7. Combination Chronological/Achievement Resume

Ronald LeBow

4071 Greenville Road	Office: (609) 555-9054
Princeton, NJ 08540	Home: (609) 555-7844

MARKETING MANAGER

Innovative, practical manager skilled in developing marketing strategies, solving problems and training sales and customer service personnel. Experienced writer, editor, platform speaker and presenter.

EXPERIENCE AND SELECTED ACHIEVEMENTS

C and S Associates
1978-present: Consultant   Princeton, NJ

Consult with clients on problems in the sales, marketing and customer service areas; prepare and present seminars for client companies; write books and training courses for publication.

- Authored comprehensive state of the art books and manuals on customer service management and operations.

- Developed and conducted on-site seminars to help clients solve specific marketing problems.

- Directed publication of unique middle management training programs incorporating multi-media techniques for a major publisher. Sales of these $1500 programs initially exceeded projections.

- Prepared and conducted over one hundred fifty seminars for managers of customer service departments. Instructed more than 2500 managers representing more than 1400 companies.

McGRAW-HILL BOOK COMPANY
1975-1979: Marketing Manager   New York, NY

Managed activities of the department, including planning and budgeting, staff assignments and scheduling of exhibits and promotions. Planned catalogs, estimated development time and costs, assigned advertising and promotional projects. Evaluated potential acquisitions and conducted feasibility studies. Worked with editorial department on packaging. Made presentations at national conventions and for major accounts. Developed sales training materials and made arrangements for sales training sessions.

- Developed campaign for winning state adoption of text-books, resulting in sales of over $25 million.

- Instituted standardized cost analysis procedures for determining project feasibility, cutting by 30% the non-productive time and costs charged against the project.

- Instituted new procedure mandating yearly evaluation of existing product lines. Removing unprofitable books from list cut warehouse and other carrying charges by $155,000 the first year.

- Produced award winning catalog cited for excellence of both graphics and copy.

1973-1975: Product Manager   New York, NY

Managed advertising and promotion for secondary reading product. Developed sales strategies and related materials. Prepared sales demonstration kits. Determined economic stocking levels. Presented sales training and educational seminars. Devised product packaging. Planned and staffed displays for national conventions.

- Increased market share and doubled product line sales to $5,000,000 by selling instructional systems rather than books.

- Conceived and installed a system for writing sales proposals, dramatically cutting preparation time and resulting in increased big ticket sales.

- Executed low cost crash development of product line, saving estimated $95,000 in development costs by getting product out by the beginning of the school selling year.

1970-1973: Educational Consultant   Houston, TX

Conducted seminars, developed training materials and sales proposals, made high level sales presentations, managed free lance consulting staff.

HOUSTON AUDIO-VISUAL SERVICES
1962-1970: Sales Manager   Houston, TX

Sold and serviced audio-visual equipment and related film-strips, cassettes and books. Managed warehouse and repair staff as well as hiring and training sales staff.

- Originated profitable training seminars leading to improved customer relations and increased sales.

- Recruited, trained and directed a professional consulting staff which charged to conduct workshops and seminars, enabling the company to turn a required activity from a loss into a profit.

- Exceeded area market projections with new product line, earning national "Top Ten" status with sales.

1959-1962: Sales Representative

Introduced audio-visual product line to the educational market in southeast Texas. Won national sales recognition award.

EDUCATION

North Texas State University   M.A.
University of Illinois   B.A.

Numerous business and management short courses and seminars.

PROFESSIONAL MEMBERSHIPS

International Customer Service Association
American Marketing Association

PERSONAL

Will travel, relocate

Letter Resumé

Each letter resumé is prepared individually for a specific target. Use the list of achievements you have in your notebook (or in your computer) to write the resumé. You can write it in standard letter paragraph form. In the regular letter form, you begin with a statement expressing interest in the job and a reason why you're a good candidate for the position. Then you continue with the accomplishments, background and experience you have that meets or exceeds their requirements. Figure 7.8 illustrates a letter resumé put together this way.

Figure 7.8. Letter Resumé

Subject: Personnel manager position

As the Personnel Manager of an international company with over 125 offices in the U.S., I developed expertise in the various areas your position requires. Much of my work was diverse and general. But as part of my responsibilities, I functioned as the EEO and Affirmative Action Director. In this role, I was responsible for writing the Affirmative Action Plan for our corporate headquarters in New York, which was then transferred to offices in all regions of the U.S.

I successfully defended the company's $1,000,000 annual government contracts when the Office of Federal Contract Compliance Programs (OFCCP) selected the company at random for an on-site review of our staff and records. The OFCCP was satisfied that the company was currently achieving equity in its hiring and promotion practices, although the company hadn't always been EEO and Affirmative Action conscious.

I interacted with divisional vice-presidents, managers and employees nationwide. Since my recruiting and selection experience is very diversified, I was frequently asked to help them on particular recruitment and hiring needs for their divisions. I established many contacts with excellent recruiting sources, some of which are not well known but supply superior candidates without fee. By using these sources, I was able to cut recruiting costs 44 percent annually in the New York area alone. I also improved targeting of quality candidates and reduced search time by creating a multimatrix resumé system.

My other human resources experience includes both labor and employee relations. I am a self-starter, am able to work independently and as part of a group and have excellent interpersonal and communications skills.

Please call to explore further how my skills will benefit you. I look forward to meeting with you at your convenience.

Sincerely,

As an alternative, you can write a letter resumé in much the same form as you would a standard resumé, but with a letter heading, a subject line indicating the job you're applying for, a summary statement (like a thumbnail) mentioning particularly the background, strengths or experiences asked for in the advertisement plus other strengths you possess that might be valuable to them. Then, you list your accomplishments, work experience and education much as you would in a regular resumé. You end with a paragraph expressing interest in the position and asking for an interview, a closing and your signature.

Testing and Revising Your Resumé

A resumé is ineffective unless it's well presented. It should be imaginatively conceived. It should advertise what you have to sell. Put yourself in prospective employers' shoes and test your completed resumé to see if it meets their standards. Will they want to see you after they read it?

Put your emotions to bed. Look at the resumé with fresh eyes:

1.   Does the thumbnail sketch mirror the experience shown in the rest of the resumé? Do the achievements or experience substantiate each assertion included in the thumbnail?
2.   Does the experience section read smoothly, continuously and logically? Or do some of the statements seem

   □   out of context, as though they belong some other place?
   □   irrelevant to the theme of the resumé as a whole?

    □   too technical, too precise, or conversely, too general and imprecise?

3.   Does the person behind the resumé become increasingly clear as you read? Or is the image blurred from time to time by statements that don't seem to fit the rest of the picture?

4.   After the resumé is read, is there a single, clear image presented? Is this the image of someone you'd like to meet?

Did your resumé meet the acid test? Is it apt to open doors?

Evaluating Different Parts of the Resumé

Now, come back and look at each part of the resumé by itself. Leave the beginning—the thumbnail sketch—until after you've evaluated the other sections of the resumé.

Achievement Resumé. Begin by reviewing the *Selected Achievements* section. Evaluate each statement in the section, using the following criteria:

1.   Do your accomplishment statements begin with action words? Does each statement include the result? Do the results include measurements of success (dollars, time, qualifying adjectives, percentages, other numerical values)?

2.   Does each statement list only accomplishment and a related result? If you've included more than one accomplishment in a statement, consider splitting it into two or more accomplishments. Or, use subdivisions under the main statement to show that a single activity resulted in multiple accomplishments and results.

3.   Have you written the statements in forceful, simple language? Or do they contain jargon, technical words or abbreviations which might not be universally understood?

4.   What about the order of the accomplishments? Do you have a strong accomplishment at the end as well as at the beginning? (Some knowledgeable recruiters read achievement resumés from bottom to top because they feel applicants put their lesser achievements at the end.) The usual order is to put the best achievement first, the next best second, the third best last, then

distribute the others evenly in between.

5. Do you have too many or too few accomplishments? Somewhere between five and eight is about right. If you have more solid accomplishments than these, you may want to write different resumés emphasizing different aspects of the job. (Whatever you do, don't throw away any good accomplishment statements. Save them in your notebook for possible use in writing cover letters or letter resumés.)

After you've finished the Selected Achievements section, go on to review the other sections, which are much the same for every kind of resumé. (Turn forward a couple of pages to find how to evaluate these sections.)

Chronological Resumé. Begin by reviewing the section you titled *Background and Experience, Relevant Experience* or *Experience.*

1. Are your positions listed in reverse chronological order?

2. Did you write the description of your duties, responsibilities and functions of your last position in the present tense? (Even when you're not working, you want to imply that you are. Using the present tense is not deceitful. For all practical purposes, that's what you still are.)

3. Have you described the other positions you had in the past tense?

4. Have you described your experience in short sentences? In simple and forceful language? Does each statement begin with a strong verb? Do the statements show that you managed, delegated, planned, organized, developed or otherwise controlled your job? Or do your statements make your performance sound passive and low level? (You assisted, helped, participated in, represented, handled.) Or worse yet, did you use nouns to describe the position rather than strong active verbs?

5. Does your record show increasing duties and responsibilities?

6. Are the descriptions of the most recent positions longer than those for earlier positions? (Most recent positions could have five or six lines of description, although three or four lines is better. Earlier positions should be described in no more than two or three

lines.)

7. What about the order of the functions, duties or responsibilities within a statement about a position? Did you put the most important aspects of the job first, and the less important or less time-consuming aspects later?

8. Did you include descriptions for only the last 15 to 20 years? (If your entire working life was with one company, include it all.)

Evaluating the Remaining Sections of your Resumé. Now look at each section you've included in the resumé. With an achievement resumé, especially one you're trying to get on one page, you may have included only Education, Business Affiliations and Personal headings. In a chronological resumé, you may have included other headings. Consider if the section should even be in the resumé. Does it contain enough information to be useful? Does it add to the picture of your competence? Have you listed your business affiliations in reverse order, most recent to most distant? Have you listed too many of these? (You need only go back 15 to 20 years.)

Have you listed your education in reverse order? (Remember, this is something employers will check.) Do you need to include any short courses or seminars to validate some of your claims? (Don't put in too many as they seem to call attention to shortcomings.) Have you earned any special licenses or registrations?

Do you need all of the information you've put in the Personal section? The catchall term "Will travel/relocate" is often enough. Don't restrict your job opportunities by listing "Houston area only," even if that's true. Don't mention marital status unless you're interested in applying for overseas positions which don't have family housing and are available to singles only. If you have any special abilities or skills which might be of value on the job, include them. Example: Speak Italian, Spanish and French; have traveled extensively in Europe, South America and the Far East. Omit hobbies and membership in social or community organizations—unless you've done something in a community organization that might strengthen your job bid. For instance, chairman of United Fund Campaign, president of Chamber of Commerce.

Should you have included any other sections? Have you received business honors or published articles or books? Do you hold any patents? If so, include the most important in a category you call Honors and Publications, *Honors and Awards, Publications, Patents* or whatever fits your situation. If you list something in a publications, honors or patent section, you're listing an achievement. Don't cover that same achievement under Selected Achievements. Don't list all of your publications by name and journal or publisher. Give titles only on those most relevant to the job you're looking for, and include the others in a catchall statement, and "numerous others in the area of —————."

Do you have any professional affiliations (job-related organizations only) which add to your stature? Do you have an office in the organization or have you held one? If you do, consider adding a Professional Affiliations heading.

The Thumbnail Sketch. The thumbnail sketch is the first thing the recruiter will read after your name and address. In fact, it may be the first thing since many don't bother with names and address unless they're really interested. Check the following:

1. Does your job title match the content of the thumbnail sketch? Does it fit the information—the accomplishments and/or achievements—given in the rest of the resumé? Is it too broad or too specific?

2. Does the content in the sketch give the reader a good summary of your skills and abilities?

3. Would it make a good advertisement?

4. Does it fit with the rest of the resumé? Is each statement substantiated by a related achievement or experience?

5. Are the statements in the sketch concrete and descriptive? Or are some of them flowery and abstract? Do any seem like puffery?

6. Are the different statements in the sketch written in parallel form? Or have you used verbs to describe your abilities in some statements and nouns in others? (This is a technical point, but can contribute to a lesser impression if you've mixed nouns and verbs incorrectly.) If you're not sure, ask someone whose knowledge of grammar you trust to review your resumé for just this point.

7. Are there more than 40 words in the sketch? What can you

leave out? How can you condense?

8. Are related skills and abilities tied together? Does the writing carry you along from one set of skills to the next or does something feel jarring or out of place?

Group Critiques of your Resumé

In job search clubs and organizations, one of the really helpful activities is what's known as a "Job Jury." Essentially, this is a group critique of your nearly finished resumé by people with similar backgrounds and experience. The purpose of this critique is to improve your resumé, to polish the wording, and to be sure you've included the most important aspects of your work life in your resumé—that you've "put your best foot forward." If you don't belong to a job search group, you can still get the benefits of group thinking by setting up your own job jury.

Ask four to six friends, former associates or people you know who have jobs that are similar to yours if they'd be willing to meet with you and help critique your resumé. Invite them to your home, or to a public place where you can have some privacy. You may want to include a meal or some other social event as part of your invitation. Send each person who agrees to help a photocopy of your resumé draft.

After they arrive, begin by summarizing your experience and accomplishments, and tell them what kind of position you're pursuing. Then, ask them to evaluate the resumé on the basis of whether the individual statements further your job search objective. Tell them to make notes on their copies of the resumé as you go and give them to you when you're finished so you can have the full benefit of their thinking. Take full and complete notes on your copy of the resumé as you go.

Regardless of the kind of resumé you're having critiqued, hold the thumbnail sketch for last. Begin with the accomplishments or the experience section, depending upon the resumé form. As the group works, you may want to bring out some of the points you learned for self-critique.

Questions to ask them to keep in mind:

- □ Have I presented each one of my accomplishments effectively? Have I put them in the right order?
- □ Have I included the key functions of the jobs I had? Have I included some which are of minor importance and should be omitted? Have I given them the proper priority?
- □ Have my principal liabilities or weaknesses been played down?
- □ Is it clear what kind of job I'm pursuing?

Go over each accomplishment or experience by itself. Read the first achievement or job description. Ask if it is all right as it sits. Is the statement reasonable and believable? What could be better, what should be deleted or omitted? How could the statement be presented more strongly? If it should be reworded, how do they say it should read? Work toward consensus. If they agree, be sure you get the reworded statement written down. If they don't reach a consensus, note the most important things that were said, and work on the statement later.

Did you leave out an important achievement, or omit some important aspect of your duties and responsibilities? It's especially easy to omit very important functions on chronological resumés.

On an achievement resumé, ask about the order of the statements. Do they present the strongest statement in the existing order, or would they be better ordered in another way? If reordered, what should that order be?

Next, ask them to look at the education section. This should take just moments since the education section should be a simple listing of colleges and degrees. Follow this with each of the other sections, in turn. What have you inadvertently left out, what should you add, what should you take away? If you've considered adding another heading with additional information, explain your thinking and ask for their advice on whether to include it or not.

Finally, ask them to go back and look at the thumbnail sketch. Explain why you used a thumbnail instead of a job objective. (If you can't remember, go back and read why earlier in this chapter.) Do they think the thumbnail is descriptive of the person described in the achievements or experience? What's missing, what should be left out? How could you change the thumbnail to make it stronger? Also ask about the job title. Is it the right one to fit the resumé and thumbnail? Take notes on their comments. If they want to help you rewrite the thumbnail, do so. Otherwise, work on it later, using your notes and the ones they gave you to polish your test.

Thank them for their help. Then, send a note thanking them again for taking some of their valuable time to give you good solid advice. If you can remember a particular contribution that person made, mention it.

Final Copy

After you've finished with your personal and group evaluation, your next step is to revise and rewrite. Then after each section is polished to your satisfaction, put the various sections together in useable form.

Suggestions:

□ The resumé must be as perfect as you can possibly make it. No typos or erasures. Pay a typist to get it perfect if you can't type well. Or prepare it on a word processor or computer, correcting it until the grammar and format are exactly the way you want them. (The ideal is to use a word processor or computer and print a fresh resumé for every application, to go with every letter or to take to every interview.)

□ If you're planning a large mailing or don't have access to word processing, have your resumé typeset and printed on an offset press. Don't photocopy your resumé unless the copy machine achieves quality near that of print (no dark lines or blurs) and can copy on good quality paper.

□ Have the resumé printed on good quality bond paper in white, off white, ivory, gray, light yellow or light gold. Blues, greens and pinks somehow don't project the executive image! For a full page or longer resumé, use 8½-by-11-inch paper. For relatively short achievement resumés, though, using executive size paper (6½ by 11½) is a nice touch. That size resumé stands out from the pack. Longer two- to four-page resumes could be printed on both sides of 11-by-18-inch paper and folded instead of being printed on two to four separate pieces and stapled. The folded resume looks like a brochure and gives a nice, not overpowering appearance.

Using Letters Effectively

Often a letter is your first contact with a company. It carries the weight of your hopes and dreams. You are trying to *sell* whoever will read your letter on your capabilities—that you're someone to consider further. The operative word here is *sell*. You're trying to persuade, to convince—but without a hard sell. During your job campaign, you'll write cover letters for your resumés, letters trying to find out if employers have jobs in your area, letters asking for appointments for interviews, networking letters asking people for help or to touch base on a referral, follow-up letters and thank-you letters.

But these letters can carry the seeds of deselection if they sound stilted, use archaic expressions or out-of-date forms. And they may be a dead giveaway to your age. Why? Because current business writing is informal and conversational. But back in the "good old days," business letters were expected to be formal. You were taught an entire set of formal business expressions that may be ingrained in your writing style. Now, this formalistic style is no longer considered the best way to write. It's difficult to understand. It's too wordy, impersonal and uninteresting.

So, how do you make changes, and what are they? Read on.

Hints to Remove Age Indications from Letters
Let's start with ways to remove age from your letters first, then look at some general hints for better letter writing.

Archaic, outmoded business expressions. Traditionally, business writers used a number of utilitarian phrases which sound stilted and unfriendly today. They also sound as though you failed to stay current. In short, they tell your readers that you're not up-to-date. The quickest way to put distance between you and your reader is to fill your correspondence with these phrases. Writing in a more conversational style eliminates this distance and brings you closer to your reader.

Change this	*to this*
In reference to your letter	This letter or your letter
Subsequent to this letter	After you get this letter or later
Please advise me	Please tell me
For your convenience, I have enclosed	Enclosed
Under separate cover, please find	I am sending
Propose alternatives	Suggest alternatives
Attached hereto	Attached
As per your letter	Your letter
If you desire	If you want
It is the hope of the undersigned	I hope
May I take the opportunity to tell you	(leave out)
Enclosed herewith is	Enclosed
Per your request	As you asked
If you utilize	If you use
If you require	If you need
I would like to thank you	Thank you

Use of slang, buzz words, jargon, technical words. Certain words become fashionable in business for periods of time and writers become attached to them. They continue to use them to show they're current with the latest trends. The words are stylish for a time, but quickly become passé. The problem: when you continue to use them long after they've gone out of general usage, you're dated. And, of course, using industry-specific jargon and technical words can be a big turnoff to people in other industries or to people who don't understand the technical side (people in the personnel department, for instance).

Word choice. Use the *right* word to express what you mean. Choose the simple word instead of the complex, the concrete word instead of the abstract, the single word instead of the phrase. The writing styles of older executives are often full of the following word choices and expressions:

1. Using abstract words instead of concrete words. Abstract words deal with concepts; concrete words deal with reality—they represent something that can be seen, felt, touched or heard. Abstractions such as bad, good, nice, fine, moderate, conservative, liberal are imprecise and really don't tell anything. Instead of *bad*, why not use *defective, flawed* or *spoiled*? Instead of *good*, how about *competent, skillful, able, capable, efficient, fit, qualified*? But many writers also clutter their letters with multisyllable words that are less vivid and concrete than short, plain words. And you need more time to recognize multisyllable words than one- and two-syllable words.

Change this	*to this*
demonstrate	show
utilize	use
sufficient	enough
initiate	start
remunerate	pay
facility	plant, headquarters
substantial	large
subsequent	next
terminate	end
anticipate	expect
ascertain	find out
consolidate	combine, merge

2. Using a noun form of a word when verb form would be better. This is the bane of executive writing in general. Many executives, who should know better, will change a perfectly good and useful verb into a noun by adding *-tion, -ation, -ion, -sion, -ance, -ence,* and *-ment*. Then they'll use the resulting word in a phrase and use a weak verb like *is, are, was, were, will, took, get,*

come, have, give, provide to show action. For instance, "We took the cost into consideration before we made a decision," is not nearly as strong as, "We considered the cost before we decided."

Change this	*to this*
take into consideration	consider
make a decision	decide
come to a conclusion	conclude
take action on	act
come to a conclusion	conclude
give assistance on	assist
make an investigation	investigate
have an achievement	achieve
develop a formulation	formulate
make a classification	classify
come to an agreement	agree

3. Similarly, a word that can be used as either a noun or a verb can weaken the sentence when it's used as a noun and another verb does the action. This makes the sentence longer and wordier, too. Example: "The accomplishment of our cost reduction was made by March 25, at which time the implementation of the revised procedures was plant-wide," is very wordy and not too understandable. In simple form, this reads: "We reduced our costs by March 25 and implemented the revised procedures throughout the plant."

Change this	*to this*
make a study	study
make a purchase	purchase
effect or undertake changes	change
make an increase	increase
make a decrease	decrease

4. Making verbs out of nouns, adjectives and adverbs by adding *-ize* or *-ate* to the end of a word is equally bad. For instance: collective + ize = collectivize. Others: legitimize, randomize, systematize, incentivize, methodize; interpretate (instead of interpret) or effectuate (instead of effect). These sound smart aleck, trendy, or in the case of the *-ate* words, uneducated. A related mistake is adding *-wise* to the end of a word to attempt to condense a

complex idea into a single word. "*Profit-wise*, I made the decision to phase out that product line." "By purchasing the chemical feedstocks in advance of the price increase, I put the company in an enviable position, *material-wise*." These sound pompous and cause readers to feel writers have an overinflated sense of their own importance.

5. Using incorrect or imprecise words. Sometimes even well educated executives will choose an incorrect or imprecise word because it sounds like the one they mean. The following words are often used in letters and in resumes during job hunting. Be sure you've chosen the right one to express your meaning.

Examples:

cite/sight/site
adapt/adept/adopt
allude/elude/refer
compose/comprise
defective/deficient
attribute/contribute
biannual/biennial
despite/in spite of
economic/economical
explicit/implicit
fortuitous/fortunate
libel/liable/likely
insure/ensure/assure
ingenious/ingenuous
observance/observation

accept/except
credible/creditable
continual/continuous
complement/compliment
definite/definitive
diagnosis/prognosis
canvas/canvass
discreet/discrete
average/mean/median
forceful/forcible
insoluble/unsolvable
equal/unique/perfect
*irregardless/regardless
healthful/healthy
phenomenon/phonemena

Note: This is *not* a word.

Active Writing

Use colorful, active verbs. Another practice which dates letter writers is the form of their sentences. Writers actually make two different kinds of mistakes here. First, they use colorless and imprecise verbs. You write the verb *think* when you could use a meaty and more interesting verb such as *confirm, verify, conceive, judge, corroborate, decide, settle, resolve, surmise, discover,* or *determine*. Using any of the other words would shade the meaning of the sentence and give a much clearer picture of your intent. Some common examples of overused words and clearer, more precise substitutes:

Change this	*to one of these*
pass	proceed, stream, circulate, occur, judge
feel	believe, consider, grope, probe, touch
make	form, build, construct, fabricate, create, devise, formulate, establish, perform, force to, cause to
have	hold, control, own, possess, experience, undergo, master
get	adopt, seize, bring, catch, capture, cause to be
give	deliver, impart, surrender, yield
tell	inform, notify, appraise, acquaint, familiarize
try	tempt, persuade, urge, test, rouse, provoke

Second, older writers use too many passive verbs and passive sentences. When you're looking for a job, you're trying to tell what *you* can do. *You* should be the subject of your writing. By using passive verbs and sentences, you lose your personal claim on the action and remove yourself from the arena. For instance:

> The defective design of the pulverizer was corrected before installation by the contractor, saving $10,000.

You aren't even in the preceding sentence. The reader is left to wonder *who* corrected the design. The contractor? Notice how much clearer the meaning is in the rewritten sentence:

> I corrected the defective design of a pulverizer before the contractor installed it, saving $10,000.

But the real problem with passive verbs is deeper than this. Letters filled with passive verbs may give the reader the impression that:

1. The writer is not accepting responsibility.

2.   The writer is dull and long-winded.

3.   The writer doesn't have anything important to say and/or is uninteresting.

Why do people continue to write with passive verbs? They confuse passive writing with objective, businesslike writing. Or somewhere along the line, they were brainwashed into thinking that using themselves as the subject of a sentence is bragging.

General Letter-Writing Hints

Every letter should be grammatically correct, including spelling and punctuation, and typed error free. But this may be the toughest part of letter writing if you no longer have a secretary and are having to rely on your own skills to produce your letters. Proofread each letter to be sure no gremlin stepped on your typewriter keys. Errors cost—they make you appear careless.

The letter should be clean. If you're sending out copies of the same letter to many different people, you'll probably photocopy or offset your letter. Be sure that the copies are clear, with no smudges or "cdgcs" that show the letter was copied and no faint print (or print that squiggles).

The Salutation. Even if you're answering a blind ad, don't *ever* write: "Dear Sir or Madam," or "To whom it may concern." Use the person's name in the salutation: "Dear President——," "Dear Chairman————," "Dear Miss——," "Dear Mrs.——, "Dear Ms. ——," (when you have a woman's name without a Miss or Mrs.). If you have a job title, you can use that, "Dear Department Head." Or "Dear Sir," or "Dear Madam," are still OK. When you don't have any idea whom to address, you can leave out the salutation entirely and use a subject line. "Subject: Marketing Director Position."

Tone of the letter. Be friendly—almost the same as you would be when writing to someone you know well. The letter should sound conversational when you read it out loud and give that feeling. Project enthusiasm. Let the letter recipients feel your confidence. You *can* do the job for them!

Even if you feel desperate about getting the job, you shouldn't *sound* or read as though you are. Don't mention any outside factors that don't bear directly on the topic. Get directly to the points you want to make and leave everything else out.

Length. Keep your letters from one to one and one-half pages long and write short paragraphs. Set up the letter so that it has a lot of "white space." You know from your own experience that busy executives tend not to read anything longer than one or two pages or that looks dense and complicated. If the letter is longer, they either put it aside or skim it quickly, reading the beginning paragraph, the first sentence of subsequent paragraphs and maybe looking at the signature. Increase your readership by using little words, short sentences and short paragraphs.

Readability

Readability, or the ease with which your reader can read your letter, is made up of several factors: sentence complexity and length, vocabulary level, style, tone and so on. The average business communication should be written at about the level of a *Reader's Digest* article—about grade level 7.5 - 9.0. One of the easiest ways to check your personal level is to use the Gunning Fog Index. This index considers sentence length as a measure of sentence complexity and the number of multisyllabic words as a measure of vocabulary level.[1] Neither is absolutely true. But a high Fog index is more likely to indicate a difficult selection than a low Fog Index. Here's how to check your personal writing Fog Index:

1.   Choose several of your writing samples—about 100 words each. Count the total number of words, then count the number of sentences. Divide the number of words by the number of sentences to find the average sentence length.

2.   Count the number of words containing three or more syllables. Don't count proper names, compound words formed by combining short easy words (overcome, grandfather), or words which become three syllables because *ed, es,* or *ing* have been added. To find the percent of difficult words, divide the number of multisyllabic words by the total number of words and multiply by 100.

---

1. Adapted from Robert Gunning, *The Techniques of Clear Writing*, rev. ed. (New York: McGraw Hill, 1968), p. 38.

3. Add the average sentence length (calculation 1) to the percent of difficult words (calculation 2) and multiply this by 0.4. The result is the Fog Index or approximate reading level.

Example: If you had three passages totalling 316 words, with 21 sentences and 42 multisyllabic words, your calculations for the Fog Index would be:

1. $$\frac{316 \text{ words}}{21 \text{ sentences}} = 15 \text{ average words per sentence}$$

2. $$\frac{42 \text{ multisyllabic words}}{\substack{\text{difficult words} \\ 316 \text{ words}}} \times 100 = 13 \text{ percent}$$

3. $(15 + 13) \times 0.4 = 11.2$, the Fog Index.

This is about the top level for letters. Above that level, they take too long to read and may end up in the round file on the floor or in the "to be read" pile on some manager's desk.

A few other simple ways to check for readability without using the Fog Index:

- Rewrite any sentence that goes over two or three typewritten lines. It's too long. Try to keep sentences under 14 words, if you can.
- Keep sentences simple: no more than 20 percent compound or 40 percent complex.
- Check for multisyllabic complex words and excess words and phrases. Get rid of them.
- Use the other suggestions in the section to edit your writing.

Using Letters in Your Campaign

You can often accomplish things with letters that you can't do on the telephone or with a personal visit. As you know, managers are programmed to respond to print. They'll answer a letter where they'd simply be unavailable otherwise. The following types of letters are those which you'll find most useful in your job search.

"Fishing Expeditions"—Prospecting for Jobs

You can write two kinds of "fishing" letters. The first you write to people you already know. You write friends, acquaintances, former colleagues or members of your industry asking for suggestions which might help in your job search. Often they'll refer you to people they know or possibly even tell you about others in their industry who are hiring. These letters should be short, friendly, direct and to the point. You don't beg for help or in any way "put the arm on them." Prospecting letters are a part of your networking efforts.

Prospecting Letter

Dear Alan:

Recent cutbacks in our industry caused the XYZ Company to eliminate the department where I've worked for 10 years. While I have several possibilities for further employment within the company, none of them look like they'll have the future I would prefer. With the company's help, I'm looking for outside opportunities as a possible alternative.

Alan, I'm writing to you for help. I don't expect that you presently know of anything that might be suitable for me—but I want you to know that I'm available. You know my general background and experience. But the attached resumé gives more details. If you have any suggestions that might help me on my campaign, I'd appreciate it if you'd let me know. Perhaps you know people in other companies who might be able to give me some assistance.

If you have time next Wednesday, I'd like to come in and chat with you to get your thoughts on my job search. I'll call on Monday to see if that's convenient for you.

Sincerely,

The second kind of prospecting letter is *referral*. You write these to take advantage of leads you get from other correspondence or from personal contacts. In the first paragraph, you mention who suggested that you contact them and why, along with a brief description of what you hope to gain. You're *not* asking for a job, but for assistance or suggestions of ways you might go ahead with your job campaign. You may also, of course, ask if they have time to see you or to talk to you on the telephone.

Referral Letter

Dear Ms. Roberts:

A mutual acquaintance, Alan White of Johnson & Brown, suggested that I contact you for advice. I am presently facing an important decision on my career and am looking for a very special kind of situation in high technology. Alan tells me that you have special expertise in this area and will know what I might do to further my career objectives.

The enclosed resumé lists these career objectives and summarizes my background and experience. I realize that it's unlikely you'd have a suitable position for me in your company. However, you know the industry and the opportunities in it. For that reason, I would be very interested in hearing your thoughts about ways I might conduct my campaign. Perhaps you could give me 10 to 15 minutes of your time to discuss this.

I'll call you early next week to see if we can arrange a mutually convenient meeting.

Sincerely,

Letter Campaigns

A few years ago, letter campaigns—contacting a number of firms who might have openings for someone of your caliber and qualifications—were very popular and productive. But times are different now. It's an employer's market, and many of the managerial and professional categories are in oversupply. This is opposed to the job availability in the job hunter's market existing in the late 1960s and early 1970s. But if you've been looking quite a while, a letter campaign might prove productive with potential employers in small- and medium-size companies. The two major types of campaigns and a variation:

1. *Broadcast or "shotgun"*. In this kind of a campaign, you send out a minimum of 100 letters (500 to 600 is a better number) to a variety of companies in the geographical area or industry where you'd like to work. Address the letter to the president of the

company, a vice-president, or a division manager in small companies. In a major corporation, a letter to the chairman of the board or the president will probably be unread—or at least not answered. Write instead to a vice-president (by name) in your area of specialization, a division or department manager or an officer one or two ranks above the position to which you might aspire. Write a rather general letter listing several of your accomplishments and give a brief overview of your background. The letter is in essence a sales letter (selling you) and should have some kind of "grabber" that makes you stand out from the crowd as someone they might consider further. Since you'll be sending out so many of these letters, have them duplicated on an offset press, a very good copier or enter them into a word processor.

Disadvantages: A broadcast campaign is expensive, both in time and in postage, duplication and stationery costs. It's seldom very effective. You'd need a really dynamite letter to draw more than a one or two percent response (a six percent response would be almost unbelievable). The lack of feedback related to the amount of effort expended can be depressing.

Letter Campaign—Broadcast Letter

Dear —————:

As a procurement executive, I have a proven record of cost reduction, instituting new policies and procedures which, in one case, resulted in a cost savings of $3.5 million from the materials and equipment budget for a major project. As a company pursuing excellence and broad experience, you may be in need of a specialist who has this expertise in multiplant and multiproject purchasing, subcontracting, inventory control, scheduling and manpower forecasting.

Some of my other accomplishments:

- Negotiated a $600,000 reduction in costs from the $3.2 million package price of two gas compressors.
- Created and implemented new purchasing procedures which saved the company $300,000 and enabled it to decrease the department work force from 25 to 15 people.
- Reduced capital tied up in inventory, thus increasing operating capital by more than $3 million. To achieve this result, I cleared a warehouse, sold excess inventory and increased inventory turnover by 400 percent.

I'd be happy to discuss these and other significant achievements with you in a personal interview at your convenience.

Sincerely,

2. *Targeted or "rifle."* This type of letter is similar to the broadcast letter except that you send it to specific people in specific industries. Your letter is much less general and is not "canned." You research the companies to whom you will address the letters so that you can mention something about the company and its products or services and tie that directly to your abilities, background and accomplishments. The letters are selling letters, much as they are in a broadcast campaign.

Disadvantages: These campaigns are time-consuming and require a great deal of effort. Each letter is tailored to fit the situation, although a substantial portion of each can be "boilerplate." The response rate is better than that of a broadcast campaign, but is still low. A 10 percent response would be exceptional.

Letter Campaign—Targeted Letter

Dear——————:

Your organization is one of only a handful of companies in the Northeastern United States that could benefit from the services of a Technical Advisor on Corporate Investment Planning. Because your company's manufacturing processes are energy intensive, you are constantly on the lookout for ways to cut costs and increase efficiency.

Some time ago, I performed a careful analysis of the benefits to my company of building a cogeneration plant. As a result, the plant was built and paid for itself in 2½ years with a $250,000 per year savings in energy costs.

This was only one of many feasibility studies I conducted. Some of my other accomplishments might also be of interest to you:

- I improved the cooling of high voltage cables by burying a small-size water pipe alongside the cable. This enabled four cables to do the work that previously would have been done by six and saved $2 million in capital expenditures.
- A utility project budgeted $500,000 for a capacitor bank. I changed

some key points in the specifications and tested the modifications in a pilot project. The modifications worked, and the bank was built at half the allocated costs.
- I carried out a complete development study for a new plant site in Latin America. The development opened the way for 2,000 new jobs, brought an income of $12 million U.S. into the country and provided major sales of hardware by U.S. suppliers.

In planning new projects, I generally consider the following: How to reduce the technical and management factors to common terms that everyone involved can understand. During the planning stages, I also consider possible intangibles, human factors and vested interests that might affect the project. Then, I perform pilot plant experiments before asking the company to commit major funding.

I have a broad education with degrees in electrical engineering and physics and a doctorate in nuclear engineering. I speak Spanish, German, French, Italian and Portuguese. I have worked 10 years in Europe and Canada. In addition, I've had extensive business dealings in Brazil, Argentina, Venezuela and Columbia.

I shall be pleased to discuss my experience with you further in a personal interview.

Sincerely,

Letter Campaign—Targeted Letter

Dear Mr. Fritze:

Your company is already a leader in its field and its sales are growing rapidly. This kind of sales growth means that your sales and marketing staff will have to grow if you are to sustain the level of growth you've enjoyed so far. I'd like to talk with you about the possibility of joining your sales and marketing team in their exciting effort.

Among my achievements as sales manager and then head of the sales and marketing department are:

- Increased annual sales almost 40 percent since 1982. Sales increased $19.5 million, with 1985 profits up $1,245,000 over 1984.
- Marketed 15 new products since 1982. These products made up 34 percent of the 1985 sales.
- Freed working capital by first reviewing product profitability, then narrowing the product line to those providing the desired profit margins.
- Developed new inventory controls which decreased inventory by 11

percent even though sales increased.
- Entered new market areas (over $2,100,000 of sales in 1985).

These advances, the result of carefully made plans and team effort, occurred in a mature industry at the expense of active competitors. We accomplished this without cutting prices; in fact, some of the new products commanded premium prices.

I thoroughly researched your company, Mr. Fritze, before writing to you. I believe my experience and background are completely compatible with your situation and that I would be a real asset to you.

If you're interested in exploring the possibilities of a match further, I'd welcome the opportunity to meet with you at your convenience. I'll telephone early next week to find out if you'd like to discuss this with me.

Sincerely,

3. *Letters used as part of a combination campaign.* The response rate on a combination campaign is better than for either a broadcast or targeted campaign. You send a letter much like what you'd send in a broadcast campaign—but you end the letter with a paragraph that says something like: "I'll call you next week to see if we can discuss this further." Then next week, you telephone and ask to talk with that person. Your chances of at least getting to talk are substantially better than if you try to call them cold. Should a receptionist or secretary answer when you call, you might say something like, "This is in reference to the letter I sent Mr. or Ms. ————— last week." You'll almost always be put through.

Responding to Advertisements

In the employer's market of the past few years, advertisements in a major newspaper like the *Wall Street Journal* drew as many as 500 to 1,000 responses. Depending upon the general state of the economy, ads will continue to draw sizable responses. Should you ignore the ads and not respond? No. The job offers are legitimate. But this depth of response does mean that your letters and resumés must be outstanding just to survive the selection process so that they'll be read by the people who'll be doing the hiring. Begin by analyzing the advertisement, then write the kind of letter which best fits the ad.

Letter resumé. When the advertisement is very specific and gives exact job requirements, a letter resumé is generally the best response. You analyze the ad, making a list of all the requirements. Then in the letter, you list each requirement and follow it with your relevant background, experience or accomplishments. If you think of ads as having personalities, this kind of detailed ad is a High S or High C ad, and should be answered specifically. You can write the resumé in a standard paragraph form. Or you can make a chart, listing the requirements in the left-hand column and matching them to your qualifications in the right-hand column. The following example shows how you might do this.

Advertisement	Summary of Requirements

Advertisement

DIRECTOR of MANUFACTURING
Ground Floor Opportunity in High-Tech Manufacturing

 pectrum Microwave Corporation is a new public company developing state-of-the-art T-1 multiplexer and digital microwave systems. We are seeking a Director of Manufacturing to organize and manage our entire manufacturing operation.

The individual we seek must be a self-starter with the following qualifications: (1) 15 years plus experience with all phases of manufacturing operations including experience manufacturing high volume, high technology electronic products; (2) experience in growth of manufacturing operations from start-up to $50 million in 3 years; (3) detailed knowledge of automatic and semi-automatic manufacturing techniques; (4) proven track record of achieving outstanding bottom line results and manufacturing margins.

The position of Director of Manufacturing can lead to a Vice Presidents' position within 2 years. Compensation includes an attractive salary, a bonus based on performance and equity.

For immediate confidential consideration, please send your resume to:

Director, Recruitment
SPECTRUM MICROWAVE CORPORATION
380 Herndon Parkway
Suite 1200
Herndon, VA 22070

An Equal Opportunity Employer, M/F/H.

Summary of Requirements

15 plus years of experience with all phases of manufacturing operations

experience manufacturing high-volume, high technology electronic products

experience in growth operations, from start-up to $50 million in three years

detailed knowledge of automatic and semiautomatic manufacturing techniques

proven track record of achieving outstanding bottom line results and manufacturing margins

The writer of the following letter performed exactly this same kind of analysis before he wrote his letter. In the first example, he wrote the letter to almost exactly match his analysis, then added a paragraph of additional information which gave a larger picture of his strengths.

Letter Resume Response to an Advertisement: Chart Form

Dear ——————:

Subject: Industrial Engineer position advertised in May 15 *Wall Street Journal*

You'll agree that I'm well qualified for an industrial engineering position. My background and experience fully matches the requirements you listed in your advertisement.

Your Requirements	**My Background and Experience**
Food manufacturing	Three years experience with the second largest food processor in the United States
Work measurement	Developed time standards for a new bottling line
Plant layout	Assisted in redesign of layout for a 120,000-square-foot plant
Cost analysis and reduction	Led the project team that devised a cost-saving program that reduced costs $500,000 in the first year of the program
5 years' experience	12 years' experience
BSIE Degree	BSIE Degree, University of Illinois

In the past five years, I instituted the use of computerized design and manufacturing in my company. I just finished an intensive short course in which I further updated my skills to utilize CAD/CAM in industrial engineering.

I would like to discuss my background with you in a personal interview at your convenience. At that time, we can discuss other aspects of my background which could be of equal value to you. I'll bring a detailed resumé listing all my background and accomplishments to the interview as well as complete salary information.

Very truly yours,

In the second example, the same letter is put into a more formal paragraph structure, but otherwise contains much the same information. Either way of writing is satisfactory.

Thank-You Letter

Dear Alan:

Thank you for taking the time to see me and advise me on my job search. I've been in touch with both Mr. Roberts and Ms. Bennett. I saw Mr. Roberts last Thursday and Ms. Bennett yesterday. Just as you said, they were most gracious and helpful. Mr. Roberts gave me an excellent lead on a job he knew was available in another company and Ms. Bennett helped me improve the effectiveness of my resumé when she pointed out that I hadn't included an important and currently saleable part of my experience.

I'll let you know when I get a new position. In the meantime, I hope to see you again at the regular association meeting.

Sincerely,

2. To interviewers after an interview. Thank them for their consideration, then summarize the main points you made during the interview. If you thought of something that should have been covered during the interview, but wasn't, include that, too. Close the letter with a positive statement that you'll expect to hear from them soon and that you would really enjoy working for them. Even if you don't want to be considered further, write the interviewer and thank him or her for interviewing you and graciously remove yourself from contention for the position.

Thank-You Letter to Interviewer

Dear ————:

Thank you for considering me for your position as a sales engineer. I came away from our meeting with a very positive feeling about your company and my ability to work with you. My seven years' experience as a sales engineer selling and overseeing the installation of stainless steel sterile production equipment for the ABC company exactly fits me for the kind of sales and installations your company makes.

My other qualifications would also make a contribution to your company: your sales engineers are asked to prepare and submit detailed process and equipment proposals—I had a very high 78 percent close record on the proposals I submitted during the past five years. My installation and training records are also good. The testing after process start-ups were uniformly acceptable. And the manufacturing and maintenance people were able to operate and maintain the lines without callback because of the effectiveness of the training I provided.

You said that the decision on those who would be interviewed further would be made by September 2. I'll expect to hear from you then.

Yours truly,

If you felt your interviewer didn't think you were qualified for the job, or the interview was generally unfavorable, you can take advantage of your thank-you note to say you're still interested in the job and bring out additional reasons why you think you should be considered and could provide the kind of services the company wants. For instance, in the following letter, a personnel manager made several points which she felt might gain her further consideration even though the interviewer had obviously been looking for someone with specific experience.

Thank-you Letter Sent After an Unsuccessful Interview

Dear ————:

Thank you for the interview on Wednesday, November 30. You're right, my experience in labor relations is limited. However, my commitment to employee relations is 100 percent.

I'm a quick study, an avid learner, and eager to work with managers and staffers to resolve problems. My experience with both the Wire Service Guild and the United Telegraph Workers' unions has given me great exposure to resolving grievances in a practical way.

We did have the advantage of solving problems occasionally by transferring staffers. However, that is costly, not always workable, and certainly not the only way to resolve an issue. We all work within the framework which exists in our company, whatever that is. Your company has options available to it that United Press International did not have.

That you have a staff devoted to employee relations says that you are sincere about your company's relations with its employees. I share your sincerity. I would bring to the Employee Relations Representative position a commitment to excellence. I believe I could further improve your employee relations program and deal with your employees in a positive, practical and open way.

I look forward to hearing from you.

Sincerely,

Letters of acceptance. You've received a job offer. A formal notice of acceptance simply states your willingness to accept the position at the salary offered, and lists what that is as well as what other perquisites were offered. It should also state when you can begin work.

Letters of rejection. You write these when you can't or don't want to accept a job offer. The key is to refuse the position graciously so that you don't antagonize the person who made the job offer. Things might change in the future, and you might want them to consider you again at a later date.

Informational letters. These run the gamut from letters giving names and addresses of references to information on your plane schedule when you're flying in for an interview. The only advice: keep the letter short and courteous; include only necessary information and don't try to write an omnibus letter.

Letter Resumé Response to an Advertisement:
Standard Paragraph Form

Dear————:

Subject: Industrial Engineer position advertised in May 15 *Wall Street Journal*

I believe that my background and experience fully matches the requirements you listed in your advertisement, and that you'll agree that I'm well qualified for your industrial engineering position.

I have had three years of recent experience with the second largest food processor in the United States. While I worked for them, I developed time standards for a new bottling line and assisted in redesigning the layout for a 120,000-square-foot plant.

In my last position, I led the project team that devised a cost-saving program that reduced costs $500,000 in the first year of the program. One of the ways we did this was to install computer-assisted design and manufacturing programs and train project members in their use.

I hold a BSIE Degree from the University of Illinois. I've recently updated my design and manufacturing skills with an intensive short course in using advanced CAD/CAM programs to shorten design time and cut design and manufacturing costs.

According to the advertisement, you're looking for someone with a minimum of five years' experience. Altogether, I've had 12 years of broad-based experience as an Industrial Engineer.

I'd like to discuss my background with you further in a personal interview at your convenience. At that time, we can discuss other aspects of my background that could be of equal value to you. I'll bring a detailed resumé listing all my background and accomplishments as well as complete information on my salary history.

Sincerely,

Selling letter. Many ads don't give much information about the job in the advertisement. They may list only the job title and a little bit about the company—or be so vague that all you get is the job title and some "insinuation." If you're interested—and many of these kinds of ads are titillating—you write a letter which presents yourself in the best light, giving a few of your major accomplishments, a brief description of your strengths, along with a couple of reasons why the company should consider you. This kind of ad communicates either a High D or a High I style. You can include an accomplishment resumé with your letter or you can omit it. In either event, mention that you'll bring a detailed resumé with you when you have your interview (which you strongly request).

Response to Nonspecific Ad

Subject: Opening for Data Processing Vice-President

I spent 10 years developing computer systems in the financial industry. In addition, I managed the development teams for the past five years and organized the training programs for those who would operate the completed systems. This is an excellent background of experience that qualifies me fully for the position you are seeking to fill.

My personal accomplishments include:

· Developed major financial applications systems (DDA, telecommunications, etc.) for three multibillion-dollar financial services firms.
· Implemented profitable new products, including a computerized employee savings plan.
· Prepared and presented both summary and detailed reports to personnel with a variety of levels of technical orientation and authority.
· Translated nebulously defined needs and requests into concrete computer-based capabilities.
· Managed the development of systems on large-scale IBM mainframes with severely limited manpower resources and tight time frames.
· Understand and can use project systems life cycles.

I look forward to discussing my qualifications in more detail during an interview at your convenience.

Sincerely,

Sometimes the ads are extremely vague and include phrases or suggested requirements that are ridiculous. One ad for an accountant, for instance, asked that the applicant be a CPA and have a sense of humor! The author of the following letter responded to one such vague ad. He felt the ad called for a sense of humor, so responded in kind.

Letter Responding to a Nonspecific Ad

(The ad requirements: that the candidate be "poised, sophisticated, have a knowledge of gourmet foods, be creative, an idea generator and a sine qua non to position." The letter got an interview.)

Dear Advertiser:

By just perusing my enclosed resumé, you'll probably agree that my background is dynamic, but my expertise is in areas you're not really looking for. However, that's where you're mistaken! I'm actually a dream merchant. I make dreams come true. I fulfill the good life, whether it be a trip around the world, a villa in Italy, a romantic bottle of champagne by candlelight or an expensive meal with exotic sauces.

I entice and then permit you to partake of the good life. I sell the sizzle! I take the millionaire and the would-be millionaire and tickle their "hot button." No, I'm not in advertising, I'm just a darn good product marketer.

But, you say, there's no food marketing background. That's the irony—there is. Of course, that's what you'll want to talk to me about. But I don't just talk about good food and wine. I indulge.

I think I'm the right person for the job, and after you meet me, you'll agree.

Sincerely,

Cover letter for a resumé. Many ads ask that you send a detailed resumé. When the ad asks for a resumé, send your chronological resumé or a combination chronological/achievement resumé. If the ad doesn't ask for a resumé, you can send an achievement resumé and write a cover letter addressing any points mentioned in the ad that aren't in the resumé. And, of course, ask for an interview.

Recently, many ads have also asked for a salary history, some even strongly suggesting that no one will be considered for an interview if that information isn't included. Most employment experts suggest that you omit this information, but cover yourself by saying that you'll bring your salary history to your interview or that your past salaries were competitive with those generally paid in the industry.

Cover Letter for a Resumé

Dear ————:

Subject: Training Specialist Position

For the past six years, I've conducted training seminars in sales, customer service, supervision, business writing, listening and problem-solving. I've written both published and unpublished training programs based on sound adult learning principles. I've also trained other trainers to conduct these programs.

During my working career, I've worked as a salesperson as well as training others to sell. I've made numerous presentations before varied audiences (from sales presentations to upper-level management to informational presentations before community organizations).

The enclosed accomplishment resumé illustrates some of my other achievements. You asked for a complete salary history. My salaries have always been competitive with those of others in the industries in which I've worked. I'd prefer not to discuss the full details of my salary history in a letter, but am prepared to disclose them during an interview.

I look forward to meeting with you at your convenience. At that time, I can provide a more detailed resumé as well as any additional information (references, etc.) that you might need.

Sincerely,

Letters to headhunters and employment agencies. Most of these advertisements list only the job title or give little information about the position. Read the ad for whatever information you can get, then write the agency exactly as you would a potential employer. However, *always* include your chronological or combination chronological/achievement resumé. Don't send an achievement resumé. Your response is guaranteed to hit the wastebasket or be ignored if you include an achievement resumé. It doesn't have the detail these people want and need to even consider you. In fact, employment agencies and headhunters, because they are providing a service, are almost by definition High S.

Letter Resumé Sent in Response to an Agency Ad

Robert Half of New York, Inc.
522 Fifth Avenue
New York, New York 10017

Subject: Controller's position advertised in the *Wall Street Journal* on November 13, 1984

The scope and responsibilities of the position outlined in this ad are of great interest to me. My experience and qualifications fully match your client's requirements. This match is shown below:

Job Requirements	*My Qualifications*
1. Supervise six employees in all phases of accounting and financial reporting	Supervised staff of 23 employees, including four accountants
2. Skilled manager	Planned workload, assigned responsibility and followed up regularly to monitor volume and accuracy
3. "Hands-on" technician	Personally performed every task, then wrote simple procedures to further train staff
4. Report to president	Prepared and submitted reports, special studies and analyses to both the president and treasurer
5. Additional strengths	Skilled in problem definition and resolution; conducted cash management program; accelerated annual audits

I'm not a CPA, but am a Public Accountant licensed by the same New York State Board that certifies CPAs. I am certified to do everything that a

CPA does except certify statements. Since companies are audited by CPA firms which perform that function, this should not be a hindrance.

I look forward to meeting with you at a mutually convenient time to discuss in greater detail your client's needs and my qualifications.

Sincerely,

Other Uses of Letters in Your Job Search

Letter of transmittal. Sometimes potential employers contact you asking for more information or a more detailed resumé. They may send a company application, a survey or a test of some kind to complete and return. Write a letter stating simply what you are sending. Include other information in the letter only if it's germane to what you're sending. Restrain your pen. The letter of transmittal could be as simple as: "Enclosed is a completed application for employment which lists all my past employers and includes the job references you asked me to supply. If you need any further information, I'll be happy to send it."

Thank-you letters. One of the biggest failings of job hunters is not to thank those who've helped along the way. You should write thank-you letters in the following instances:

1.   To people who've helped you. Send them to friends who've given you leads; to executives who've been willing to give you suggestions for your job campaign; and to receptionists, secretaries and/or assistants who've been especially nice or helpful to you when you went on an interview. These should be short, should mention what they did that you appreciated, and should be sincere.

The Interview, Part I

You've gotten a positive response from your letter or resumé—you've been asked to come for an interview. The ball is in your court. Unless the job is totally different from what you want, accept. You have a golden opportunity—if not for employment, at least a chance to practice your interview skills and learn from the experience.

From your past experience, you probably used interviews as much for deselection as for selection. To be sure, interviewers are literally looking to see whether a job candidate is a member of the "to be considered" or "not to be considered" group. So your primary goal now on an initial interview is to make it into the "to be considered" group. A job offer is seldom tendered on the first interview.

The most common interview structure within larger firms is the following: 1) an interview in the personnel or human resources department, 2) an interview by the hiring manager (the manager interviews only those applicants who "passed" the first interview and are recommended for further investigation by the personnel department) and 3) interviews with other company management. The third step may be repeated several different times with different management groups, especially when the job to be filled is a key position.

Your key to ultimate success is to show not only that you're looking for a position, but that you're ready and prepared to perform in that position. In short—you'll have to "market" yourself during the interview.

General Tips on Interviewing

In planning for an interview, think about the things you looked for when you were interviewing prospective employees yourself. What did you want to know about the candidates? What characteristics did you look for in them? You wanted to know what they'd done and how they'd done it. You were vitally interested in how they'd perform for you and you wanted to know something about them as individuals.

How did you feel as the interviewer—were you nervous, or were you able to interview the candidates without stress? The shoe's on the other foot now. You're the person looking for the job. But the interviewers on the other side of the desk are not so different from you. They're looking for the same things. They want to know *what* you've done, *how* well you'll perform, *why* you're a good prospect for the company and *who* you are as an individual.

Making Arrangements

You have an opportunity to prepare for most interviews, and you can at least partially control a number of factors related to the interview.

Timing. You can usually influence the day and time of the interview. Think back to your active employment. What days were the least hectic? Which the most? Don't set up inverviews on days when interviewers are likely to be harassed. OK. That leaves Mondays and Fridays out as interview days. Set up your interviews, then, on Tuesday, Wednesday or Thursday, if you can. Try for an appointment early in the morning, between 9 and 10 A.M. or early in the afternoon just after lunch. If these times are out, at least ask for an appointment not too late in the afternoon so that the interviewers won't be either too immersed in their job activities or too tired to conduct a fair interview.

Research the Organization. Your next move—prepare for the interview. You may already know a great deal about the prospective employer because you researched the organization early in your job campaign. Or, you may know next to nothing about it. To present yourself in the best light, you want and *need* to be informed so that you can show your understanding of the situation. You want to stand out from the pack.

So go back to some of the same sources you checked when you were preparing your job campaign. Look for information in the library, the various directories and information sources mentioned in Chapter 6.

If it's a small company, you may want to telephone the librarian at the newspaper in the town closest to the interview location. Or a new method, increasingly used these days, is to consult a computer database. You have a couple of choices here. One option is to contact companies whose sole purpose is to research companies for prospective job candidates. For a relatively small fee, you will get a complete printout on whatever information has been printed about the firm in business publications, technical journals and other media. This service can include information about competitors, what the company said in its press releases, security analysts' published information about the company's potential, information about key executives, stock ownership data and so on.[1]

A second option: in many libraries, you can use a computer to search one of the subscription databases. If you go this route, you're charged only for the computer search time, the telephone call and the printout. If you have a home computer and a modem, you can contact one of the public database services such as The Search and locate the information that way.

If you *still* don't have the information you'd like, you have a few more options. Call your interviewer's secretary or the company's public relations department to ask for information or brochures. If it's a publicly held company, ask for a copy of the annual report. At the least, find out what the company or organization does. Should this be unproductive, then ask the secretary or receptionist some questions about the company while you wait for the interview. If all else fails, ask for information during the interview. Say something like, "I couldn't locate much information about your company. But

---

1. Claudia A. Gentner, "The Computerized Job Seeker," *Personnel Administrator*, August 1984. Ms. Gentner directs such an information retrieval system at Seagate Associates, Paramus, NJ 07652.

the position sounded so interesting, I felt I just had to find out about it."

Ready for the Road

You're ready to leave for the interview. You've made the necessary changes in your wardrobe and appearance—you'll make the best impression you can. Some suggestions for getting ready:

Personal Appearance

□ Dress neatly. Be sure your shoes are polished and heeled and that your clothing matches the industry style and is in quiet, conservative colors.

□ Hair. Men, get a good haircut; women, your hair should be clean and attractively styled.

□ Women, take special care with your makeup and tone down the eye shadow and rouge. Wear tasteful, "quiet" jewelry or no jewelry. Men—no chains!

□ Hands. Prior to the interview, check to be sure you don't have newsprint on your hands from reading a paper or magazine in the waiting room. If your hands are clammy, wash them just before going in. Use an antiperspirant or spritz a mild, alcohol-based cologne on the hands to remove moisture.

Briefcase

□ Carry one if you're showing work samples or a portfolio.

□ Don't leave a copy or sample if it contains important information which would be of value to the interviewer. The company might not need you since they've already picked your brains.

□ If you're interviewing for a position where you normally wouldn't need work samples or a portfolio, don't carry them along in a briefcase. If they're interested, you'll have an "in" for another interview where you can show what you've done.

Resumés. Always carry copies of each of your different styles of resumé. Put them in your pocket or briefcase. But don't offer one unless the interviewer asks for it. Reread it in advance of the interview.

Salary history and references. In addition to the resumé, take a list summarizing your salary history and a list of personal and business references, complete with correct addresses and telephone numbers. If you're asked to fill out an application, you will need this information, too. But don't offer references to anyone unless requested. You don't want to bother your reference people unnecessarily.

An obvious, but important point. Leave early enough to get there on time! If you're driving, check the route on your map the evening before. If you've flown into an area the night before the interview, check at the hotel for some idea of the driving time and best route (should you have rented a car), or arrange for a taxi to pick you up early enough to get to the interview on time. Of course, some companies arrange for the "care and feeding" of their management-level interviewees, in which case, you'll be picked up by someone and driven to the interview on time.

The Preliminaries

Too often, you will feel as though you are running a gauntlet just to get in to see the interviewer. At a factory, you may have to check in with the guard at the gate, sign in and go through the pass or badge routine, the search-and-find mission to locate the office and so on. Especially when you're already nervous, these delays may seem interminable—but they're just part of the drill. And you have to allow for them.

OK. You're now in the area where the interview will occur and you're ready. What other delays can there be?

The secretary, receptionist, assistant to or other staff member. Be as polite and cordial to the staff as you will be to the actual interviewer. Accord them status. Above all, if the staff member is female—or for that matter, ladies, if male—don't call him or her "honey" or "dearie" or any other term which might be seen as a putdown.

Don't tell the secretary or staff member what position you will be interviewing for. Respond with something like, "I'm here to interview for a position" or "Mr. or Ms. X is expecting me."

Filling out application forms. Many companies have gotten shrewd about the use of resumés as hiring devices. Resumés don't have the force of law behind them. They're generally not signed and don't have a statement verifying their truthfulness. Therefore, companies may require even the candidates for top executive positions to complete a company employment application *before* the interview.

A reminder: Don't give wrong schooling information. This is now one of the few permissible and checkable sets of information which companies are allowed to get before you're hired. Yet a nationwide survey a few years ago showed that education was also the most lied about item on resumés and applications. However, you'd only be embarrassed if the prospective employer checked up and found out you lied on a resumé since it isn't a legal document. But an application is a legal document—if you lie on it and are found out, it's a fireable offense. Use your chronological resumé to fill the application out accurately. Be especially neat and be careful to answer all the questions. Occasionally an application form will contain illegal questions. You can choose to answer the question, fill in with the letters NA for not applicable or draw a dash across the response blank.

The wait. Use your waiting time to find out about the company, to check yourself again, to review your answers to possible interview questions. If any brochures, annual reports or advertising pieces on company products or services are in the waiting area, look at them for additional background information.

Talk pleasantly to the secretary or receptionist. You can often pick up useful information without being overtly curious. And do ask how your interviewer's name is pronounced if you're not sure.

You have no problem if you're told the interview will be delayed. But when it's more than 20 minutes late, ask how long the delay will be. Say something like, "Is Mr. or Ms. so-and-so aware that I'm here?"

Should the delay run to 45 minutes or more, you run a risk.

They've made you wait. Without any kind of rancor, comment something like, "I had an appointment at 10:00 A.M. I would like to reschedule the appointment, if possible." However, if you were flown in or drove a long distance for the interview, you must wait, rechecking every 10 minutes or so without appearing nervous. Some companies actually delay interviews as a sort of test to see how you react to and manage stress.

The Actual Interview

The order of events varies with each interview and interviewer. Remember, though, that most interviewers are predisposed in your favor. They want to hire someone—and most of the time, they'd as soon it were you. Most aren't professional interviewers. It's just a part of their job—and a part they're usually not very good at. You'll see one of three types of interviewers: (1) *Self-made individualists* pride themselves on their ability to size people up. They're sure of themselves, and conduct the interview accordingly. (2) *Inexperienced recruiters* are unsure how to begin. These are the most nervous interviewers and may spend too much time on small talk before leading up to ask the nitty-gritty questions they feel are essential. (3) *Professional personnel interviewers* know their business. They may be nondirective and low key, but they will be relevant. They'll maintain reins on the direction and pace of the interview.

Some general tips for the interview:

Handshake

- Use a strong, firm, "normal" handshake. Slide your hand into the other person's hand to avoid hitting or crunching rings.
- If the interviewer offers his or her hand, take it at the beginning. Otherwise, don't offer to shake hands yourself. Business women should also shake hands when the interviewer offers.
- After the interview is over and rapport is established, you can initiate the handshake.

Eye contact

- Look your interviewers straight in the eyes and avoid shifting your eyes away or down.
- In a group interview situation, begin by looking at the questioner, then slowly sweep around the room to include everyone in the group in your answer.
- Wear glasses if you normally do so. That way, you can see properly.

Body language

- Sit comfortably in the chair.
- Don't cross your hands over your chest. This is a blocking move. For the same reason, don't put your hands behind your head. That's an aggressive move.
- If you cross your legs, do it toward the interviewer. Keep the contact open. Then, periodically, recross your legs to avoid having them go to sleep.
- Keep your hands away from your mouth and face. This is read as a nervous gesture indicating you're unsure of yourself.
- Keep your hands down, preferably in your lap.
- Try to avoid any other nervous movements.

Don't put anything on the interviewer's desk. You may be encroaching.

Don't chew gum—or anything.

Don't lose your sense of humor in an interview. If the interviewer says something funny, laugh—or at least smile.

Formality/informality

- Don't go to a first-name basis unless the interviewer requests you do so. The interviewer may consider it disrespectful. Age can play a part here. When your first interview is in the personnel department, you frequently may be interviewed by someone who is young enough to be your son or daughter. The temptation is very strong to go directly to a first-name basis just because you're older and have a lifetime of deference from younger people. Resist the temptation.

□ Avoid using a first name if you haven't been given permission. Use the last name of the interviewer with Dr., Mr., Miss, Mrs. or Ms. But be careful with Ms.—some women don't like that term. If you'll be speaking with a woman and you don't know her martial status, either ask the receptionist or secretary ahead of time, or ask, "Is it Miss or Mrs. _____?"

□ When the interviewer has a difficult name, write the name correctly with phonetic respelling so you won't make a mistake.

Identify the interviewer's communication style. Are you faced with a High D, a High I, a High S or a High C (see Chapter 4)? Make your judgment early in the interview and modify your own style accordingly.

Don't appear to control the interview. Listen carefully, then answer questions thoughtfully. (More on this later in the chapter.)

Don't take notes on the interview, other than to be sure you've spelled the interviewer's name correctly.

Chemistry is important in an interview. But if rapport isn't there, *don't blow the interview.*

□ The chemistry may be wrong because one or both of you takes an instant dislike to the other.

□ The interviewer may remind you of someone you don't like.

Don't smoke, regardless

□ Even if the interviewer smokes, don't do it yourself. Smoking is now a deselector in many companies. They're consciously looking for nonsmokers since research on smoking employees indicates that smokers cost a company $4,611 a year more than do nonsmoking employees.[1]

---

1. Research conducted by Albert Weis, associate professor in the Allen School of Business at Seattle University and reported in *Management Review*, September 1984, p. 6.

- Smoking may interfere with your ability to handle the interview.
- Even if the other person suggests that you smoke, if you'd like, it would be better for you to abstain.
- Absolutely no cigars or pipes. Many managers and employers have a whole set of stereotypes which they falsely apply to cigar and pipe smokers.

Health. If you're asked a question about your health, answer "excellent." If you answer anything else, you can dig yourself a hole. But should you find yourself coming down with a cold or the flu, call ahead of time and tell them you're catching a cold or the flu, and ask if they'd prefer to reschedule the interview.

Interviewing tricks done by "unscrupulous interviewer" to find out your reactions to stress:

- Rocking chair. One leg of the chair may actually have been shortened to make it rock. Comment, "There seems to be something wrong with this chair." Change chairs if you can. Don't just sit there and accept discomfort.
- Don't sit on a couch if you can avoid it. Sometimes you can't do anything about this. The interviewer may have seated you on the couch thinking it will put you more at ease.
- The interviewer can put distance or height to work to your disadvantage.
- You may be seated so that the sun or a light shines in your face. Tell the interviewer that you'd like to move so that you can see him or her.

Lunch or other meals

- If you are asked to join the interviewer for lunch, go ahead.
- Don't order expensively. And don't order anything that could be messy!
- When you are asked if you'd like a cocktail and you either don't drink or don't want to drink, don't say, "I never touch the stuff." Join in by ordering Perrier or club soda with a

twist. If the others in the party are having drinks and you chose to join, stay well behind. More than that can make you slur your words or make a misstatement. But wait to order a drink until after the interviewer does. Then match the drink type and preferably, have only one. The interviewer may be checking your interest in, capacity for and tolerance of alcohol.

Follow-up after the interview. *Always* write a thank you note to the interviewer. It should be relatively brief, but you can use it to amplify important points not covered to your satisfaction, correct possible misconceptions or transmit supplemental information the interviewer requested. The thank-you letter is a superb place to summarize the interview and strengthen those two or three clincher points you want the interviewer to remember. It's also a good idea to send a thank-you note to an especially helpful secretary, receptionist or assistant.

Coping with a Stress Interview

Welcome to the stress interview. Instead of an interviewer, you've got an interrogator—you feel as though it'll only be a matter of a few minutes before "they" come and take you to be fingerprinted and have a mug shot taken.

The stress interview is the one in which you're treated as though you're the enemy. The interviewer asks you a number of offensive questions that are designed to put you on the defensive. The physical setting may also be uncomfortable—the room is full of smoke, has inadequate lighting, heating or cooling, uncomfortable chairs or too low a couch for you to sit on, or you may be asked to sit so that you have to face a bright window and can't see the interviewer's face.

In a tight job market, more and more companies use these "grilling" interviews to "separate the men from the boys, the women from the girls." They're a trick—and it's one you can learn to play.

First, don't put up with an unpleasant environment. Ask politely to sit in a different chair or to move so that you don't have to face the window. Comment on the lack of heat or cooling in a commiserating fashion. "Gee, it must be tough to have to work when the heating (or cooling) isn't adjusted for your comfort. I hope they get it fixed for you soon."

Second, refuse the invitation to go on the defensive. Practice responding to tough questions (see the list in the next chapter) so that if you're asked one, your response will be easy and relatively automatic. You want to answer them in a sincere, direct manner. You try to move through the volley of unpleasantness as fast as you can so that you can get on to the meat of the interview.

Also consider your own hot buttons. What kind of comments or questions tend to put you on the defensive? What in your background or experience could be embarrassing? What is on your resumé (or isn't on there) that might need some explanation? Prepare these answers, too. People who regularly conduct stress interviews have an absolutely uncanny ability to go for the jugular. And they'll be successful if you're not ready.

But if you've been subjected to a stress interview and handle yourself with confidence and aplomb, you'll have made a conquest. They'll be trying to get you signed, sealed and delivered.

Many people say they don't want to work for a company that would employ stress interviews. That's unrealistic. Many jobs out there are full of daily stress. It's not unreasonable for companies to want to know how you react. If you keep your cool and respond well under fire, they'll be more likely to want you. That's the kind of executive timber they have to have if they're going to survive in the tough competitive environment of today.

The Second, Third and Fourth Interviews

The second interview is really easier than the first. You've already survived the initial screening process. You know something about the company now. And, your first interviewer now has a vested interest in you. He or she has essentially said you're all right. So, you may be able to ask and get the ammunition you need to make it safely through the next interview.

With lower-level employees, the job offer is typically made on or after the second interview. But with mid- and top-level executives and managers, four and five interviews before hiring are not uncommon.

If the first interview was with someone in personnel, the second interview will probably be set up with the person to whom the position will report. If this is the case, you might call the original interviewer and ask if there's anything you should know before you meet with the next interviewer. You can also ask if there are any objections if you make a direct call to the interviewer before you come in.

Since there will usually be no objection, call the second interviewer. Say something like, "I'm looking forward to meeting with you on (*date*). Would you like me to prepare anything in advance or bring anything special to our meeting? If you get specific requests, then bring them along in your briefcase. In any case, you've introduced yourself pleasantly to your interviewer, acknowledging that you're ready to do whatever you can to enhance your chances.

A second interview can take the same track as a first interview. Or it can be entirely different. It depends upon who's interviewing you and whether this will be someone to whom you'll be reporting or will be someone higher up. If it's the person to whom you'd be reporting, expect the interview to be more direct and job related. If it's a higher up, you may have a relatively general interview in which you'll be expected to talk about your personal goals and objectives, about the company's goals and objectives, its bottom line, and about what contribution you could make to meeting those goals and objectives.

Ask the first interviewer if he or she is going to introduce you to the second interviewer. When the answer is affirmative, on arrival, ask the first interviewer for a briefing on what you can expect. You'll get an idea at least of the timetable, and may gain a valuable insight, which will help you. Also, when you're introduced by someone else in the company, you get a little bit of rub-off halo. That will get the interview off to a friendly start, and the second interviewer may be predisposed in your favor.

One other thing. Before the second (and subsequent) interviews, ask for annual reports, brochures, descriptive information, catalogs, and any other information sources they have. Then bone up thoroughly on the company before you come in. You'll give better and more informed responses. And they'll be impressed by your interest in them and attention to detail.

The Interview, Part II: Handling Questions

You know that the direction an interview takes depends largely on whether a staff-recruiting interviewer (say someone in the personnel department) conducts it or whether it's handled by the person who'll be the superior in the reporting relationship. Staff experts may not be able to judge your exact skills, but can size up your experience, interpersonal skills, ability to communicate and the way you handle yourself during the interview. These experts now conduct the initial interview for even high-level positions and maybe, in your own experience, handled the initial interviews of your own staff hiring. Now, they'll compare you with the other people they've screened and make recommendations for further interviewing. They're important to your job search and you *have to get past them to go further*. They usually ask general questions, and don't get into technical details. They're trying to answer the unasked questions: "How much are you worth to my company?" and "How good can you make me look?"

Line managers, on the other hand, frequently skip the general questions. They get directly to the nitty-gritty and start the interview with questions they think will determine whether your qualifications fit the specifics of the job or not.

Techniques to Keep the Interview under Control

For years, you've been on the other side in the interview situation. You may feel that you know everything you need to know about interview communications and interactions. But please read this section just for the review value. It's always different from the interviewee's angle. And, there just may be something in this section that's new to you that you can add to your bag of skills.

An interview is a communication interaction between you and the interviewer. Both of you want to present yourself in the best possible light and want the interview to be successful. Some of the communications skills that will help you bring your interviews to a successful and desired conclusion include asking and answering questions to get and give information while still presenting what's most beneficial to you and being able to summarize the topics covered during the interview (this is a device that helps you keep the interview on a track that's favorable to you). You should also be able to listen carefully to the interviewer, to "read between the lines" and think along with the interviewer so you don't miscommunicate.

You can present yourself favorably by: 1) determining what skills, background and experience are needed to fill the position, 2) showing how your skills, background and experience match or exceed those needs and 3) demonstrating how hiring you can benefit the interviewer's company. This technique is known as the *Needs/Benefits Link-Up*. It's widely used by salespeople when they're selling products and services. And, of course, that's what you're doing during an interview—you're selling the benefits of your services.

Question and Answer Techniques

Chapter 9 ended with a suggestion that you practice in advance by going through mock interviews with friends, family or other unemployed executives. What you want to develop is your ability to answer the really tough questions (see the last part of this chapter). You also want to hone your ability to parry unwanted questions and to ask yourself for the information necessary to evaluate the company, the position and any offer.

The general purposes of questioning are: to collect information, to evaluate how someone thinks or feels, and to confirm facts and attitudes uncovered by other questions or sources. Both you and the interviewer use questions to build rapport, understand the situation and move the interview along. Questions come in two major forms, open-ended and closed. Open-ended questions allow answerers to give free responses and to direct responses into areas of concern to them. They often begin with who, what, when, where, which, how, or why. Either you or the interviewer can direct open-ended questions to a wide variety of uses:

- □ to open conversations and provide background
- □ to ask for information
- □ to follow-up, to ask for elaboration
- □ to probe for causes, additional or related information
- □ to check understanding, determine awareness of pros and cons
- □ to ask for reasons why (Why do you suppose...?)
- □ to ask for suggestions
- □ to determine sources
- □ to check knowledge or memory

Closed questions, on the other hand, are questions that have only one answer. They can be answered with a "yes" or "no." You use these to narrow your field of inquiry, to get confirmation, and to determine that you're on the right track with your questions.

Closed questions usually begin with some form of the verbs *be, do* or *have*; is, are, were, isn't, aren't, weren't; do, does, don't, doesn't; have, has, haven't and hasn't. They can also begin with should, would, will, won't and so on.

The following examples illustrate the differences between open-ended and closed questions:

Open-ended Questions

Have you ever had any hobbies that would help you perform well in this position?

What can you tell me about yourself that makes you think you're a good salesperson?

Based on what I've told you about this organization, why do

you think you'd like to work for us?

How do you feel about the hours?

Closed Questions

Do you understand what this job entails? (This is a question calling for a "yes" or "no" response. However, you would do better, if you're asked this one, to answer "yes" or "no," then continue either with a summary of what you understand or a pointed question of your own to clarify what you don't understand.)

Did you have enough opportunity for advancement in your last job?

Do you think you could work for a younger person?

In addition, you may ask or be asked semiopen questions which have only one answer, such as: "When can you begin work," or "Which do you prefer, a straight salary or a lesser salary plus a bonus tied to your performance?"

You'll both answer and ask general and specific questions. Interviewers use general questions early in the interview to open topics, to begin exploring areas of common interest and to define areas of concern. They use specific questions later to focus on details, gather specific information and verify understanding. And you will ask the same kinds of questions of your interviewer, although to begin with, you're more likely to be the responder than the asker.

Two kinds of questions are particularly important to you. The first are *Strategic Questions*. They're primarily offensive weapons. You use them to uncover information about the employer's needs and attitudes. For instance, if the interviewer says something like, "I'm afraid you're overqualified for this position," a strategic question for you to ask would be "The word 'overqualified' puzzles me. Why do you say that, Mr. Ellis?" You ask a question, going on the offense, rather than becoming defensive. A strategic question, then, keeps you in charge. At the same time, you gain enough information about the needs and attitudes of the employer to deal productively with the situation.

The other kind of questions you'll use are *Tactical Questions*. Tactical questions are primarily defensive weapons used to sidestep or parry difficult or nuisance questions and to shift the psychological initiative from the interviewer to yourself. An example of the way you might use a tactical question: The interviewer asks one of those really tough questions, such as, "Why did you leave your last job? In the last 10 years, you've worked for several companies."

Rather than answering the question outright, turn the conversation back on the interviewer by asking something like, "You mean you're concerned about the fact that I've held several jobs recently?" After the interviewer responds, you could go into the reasons behind the various jobs, particularly if you took them to learn something new, you lost them through mergers or because you'd finished your assignment. (Particularly true for engineers and technical people.)

Both strategic questions and tactical questions can be used at any point in the interview where they seem appropriate. And they can be either open-ended or closed.

Interviewer: This job requires a real specialist. The right person for the job must have the right kind of training and experience.

Job Applicant: What kind of training and experience would that be, Mr. Murray? (open-ended, strategic question)

Interviewer: We won't make our final decision until after we've interviewed the two other candidates who fit our initial specifications. It should take us a little while longer.

Job Applicant: Do you plan to make your final decision by the end of next month? (closed, strategic question)

Needs/Benefits Link-Ups

As soon as you can in the interview, you want to tie in your skills, background and experience to your potential employer's needs. In short, you should be able to link an employer's needs to the benefits your qualifications offer in a persuasive statement. For instance, if the interviewer explained that they're looking for someone with experience in planning and starting up an automated factory, you might say something like:

> Mrs. Baker, you need someone with experience in installing and operating an automated factory. On my last position, I evaluated the existing production system at the XYZ company. On the basis of that evaluation, we completely revamped the production lines, retaining and automating what equipment we could salvage and installing the needed new equipment. We retrained existing personnel rather than hiring technicians from the outside. After the production lines were in full operation, we increased production 275 percent, improved quality and cut the reject rate, while at the same time, we were able to reduce unit production costs.

This statement illustrates the two steps of a good Needs/Benefits Link-Up Statement. It began with a brief statement of the employer's need. Then it continued with related benefits your qualifications could provide. (The statement referred to several related benefits.)

Another example:

> Mr. Forbes, Charles Peck from University Associates told me that you're looking for someone with a background in specialty chemical sales and sales management to head up your new telemarketing department. I sold specialty chemicals and was a regional manager for 10 years with Reem and Speas. In addition, I started a telemarketing operation three years ago, which increased our sales substantially with marginal customers.

Look for opportunities to use Needs/Benefits Link—Up Statements, and use one as soon as you have a reasonable opportunity to do so. You'll do this as soon as the interviewer finishes a preliminary statement describing the position. You want to make your statement agree with the interviewer's definition of the job. You may find opportunities to make several different Needs/Benefits Link—Up Statements during the course of an interview, showing how different aspects of your abilities could benefit the employer.

Summaries Keep Interviews on Track

One of the best ways to build empathy and understanding is to periodically summarize or paraphrase the meaning or main idea of different parts of the conversation. That way, you can: confirm that you understood what was said, define an attitude or restate a fact, place a statement of the interviewer on record. You use a *Confirmatory Paraphrase* for that purpose. Or, you can use a paraphrase to suggest disagreement without actually contradicting the interviewer or force the interviewer to reexamine a previously stated position or premise. You use a *Leading Paraphrase* for this second purpose.

When you make a Confirmatory Paraphrase, use some of the interviewer's same words, almost like an echo. Or, rephrase completely, using your own words to summarize the gist or main thought. When you're getting an intuitive message, one that's not stated in words, but implied, trying a Confirmatory Paraphrase can let you off the hook. It allows you to ask for verification of what you've felt but which wasn't said.

Example of a Confirmatory Paraphrase:

What you're looking for, then, is someone to revamp the department, cutting down on expenses while continuing to maintain high standards.

In this position, then, I'd be expected to introduce new product into existing markets, increase the sales on your current products and help open new markets.

A Leading Paraphrase, on the other hand, summarizes something which has been said, but does it in such a way that it brings the interviewer's position into question. Imagine, for instance, that you've applied for a position in the business school of a state university. They're looking for someone with business experience, a master's degree and ability to make presentations to local businesses. You have all of the stated requirements, in addition to years of business—training experience. In your conversation with the interviewer, it suddenly dawns on you that they're interested only in a local person with an MBA (preferably from their institution) and aren't really interested in considering anyone with an MS or MA degree regardless of background and experience. A Leading Paraphrase might be:

> If I understand you correctly, it's more important to you that the person filling this position be local and have an MBA than that they have a proven business record and experience in making presentations before large groups.

A Leading Paraphrase is a good way to begin countering the age question. For instance, if an interviewer comments, "Your background is certainly impressive and you have the breadth of experience we need for the position. But, to be honest, we were looking for someone younger to fill the position."

A Leading Paraphrase response would be something like, "Oh, you feel that my background and experience are less important to your company than my age?"

You'll use other kinds of summaries during the interview. Summaries are useful, for instance, to get an interview back on track after the interview has been interrupted for some reason. Summarize briefly the topic of conversation that was interrupted. Then, continue in the line you'd like the conversation to go in. You can: 1) reemphasize and expand upon the remark you made just prior to interruption; 2) redirect the conversation into other channels; or 3) ask the interviewer a question to obtain information you'd like to have.

> Just before your secretary interrupted us, you'd asked me what experience I'd had managing a clerical staff. In my last position, in addition to managing a staff with 15 accountants and two lawyers, I also managed three secretaries, a file clerk, a person who did word processing and a receptionist.

Before the telephone rang, we were talking about the lack of up-to-date written corporate policies and procedures. Is one of your goals that these be revised and developed for this division?

When the interview ends, you want to have a reasonably firm understanding of what the next step will be. Frequently, interviewers clearly state what they have in mind and make some kind of commitment. But if they don't——they've made no offer or haven't suggested a second meeting——or they've stated a conclusion that's unacceptable to you, you'll want to try an *Interview Conclusion Statement*.

In an Interview Conclusion Statement, you begin with an assumptive summary of at least two important benefits which the company would get if they hired you. You *assume* that the interviewer recognizes the value of those benefits. Then you would continue by requesting some kind of commitment, even if it's just for another meeting with a different interviewer——perhaps another manager mentioned by the interviewer. The request for commitment should be appropriate to the situation, and is usually not a push to try to get the interviewer to commit to hiring you.

Mr. Adams, we've agreed that my recent hands—on experience with computer auditing is the kind of experience that your company is looking for. Also, my experience in working with outside audit firms would be useful to you in cutting down on the time and expense of your annual procedures. When might it be convenient for me to speak with your Chief Financial Officer?

In the example, there's no element of pleading and there's a definite request for further action. Note the difference in wording and in effect between the example above and the poor interview conclusion statement below:

Mr. Adams, if you feel my qualifications in auditing are adequate, perhaps I could call you next Tuesday to see whether or not I could meet with your Chief Financial Officer.

Questions to Answer and Ask
According to James E. Challenger, president, Challenger, Gray

& Christmas, a national Chicago—based outplacement consulting firm,

> The strategy for success in an employment interview is to be whom the interviewer wants you to be. It is done by listening for clues as to what he or she wants and responding with the appropriate answer.

> All interviewers are seeking the answer to the basic question of why they should hire you as opposed to at least six other candidates who are equally qualified. How well you address yourself to their image of the ideal candidate will usually determine whether or not you get the job offer.

Questions You Should Be Able to Answer

The key to success or failure in a competitive employment interview often hinges on how you answer five questions. Challenger lists these questions and tells why your answers are important:[1]

1. *"Why are you interested in us?"* Most jobs that job seekers accept have not been publicized and may not even have been created yet when the job seeker comes to call. Rather than answer how you can fit in, tell the interviewer how good you are at what you do and demonstrate that you are so well qualified that the company cannot do without you. Let them figure out how you can best fit into their plans.

2. *"Tell me about your current and previous employers."* Don't criticize current or former employers because it will reflect unfavorably on you. But don't go to the other extreme and give your superiors all the credit for your professional development. Take as much credit for what you've done as you can. This is what impresses the interviewer.

3. *"Tell me about your strengths and weaknesses."* Concentrate on the strengths and avoid the weaknesses. Even a seemingly harmless statement such as "lack of patience with inefficiency" is

---

1. From a press release, June 25, 1984.

dangerous. It can be read as a sign that you have a quick temper, are hard on subordinates or can't handle a difficult situation without losing your cool.

4. *"What are the best and worst aspects of your present (or last) job?"* As far as you are concerned, there are no worst aspects. It's much better to talk in terms of challenges that have confronted you and what you did to meet those challenges.

5. *"Tell me something about yourself."* Responding correctly to this directive is the most important to your success. Think in terms of what the interviewer wants to hear. He or she wants to know how good you are, but also if there is anything about you that could cause problems. Avoid the latter.[2]

In many respects, Challenger's questions are the easy ones. As an unemployed older executive, the toughest questions are those which go for the jugular——the questions that may show an age bias or touch on an emotional nerve, say why you're not currently employed. For example:

□ Could you work for a younger man (or for a woman)? Have you ever done so? (Your answer——I can work for anyone as long as there is mutual respect and that person knows the job.)
□ Why did you leave your last job? (This one is really tough. You have to tell the truth, but in a way that puts neither you nor your former employer in a bad light.) If you happen to get a really nasty interviewer, this question might even be couched something like: If you were so good over there, why did they let you go?
□ How long have you been out of work now?
□ Aren't you overqualified (or too experienced) for this job? (For this answer, you'll have to stress your qualifications against a younger candidate. Point out that experienced executives are at a premium today. And, because you're experienced, it will take you less time to become proficient in the job.)

---

2. Ibid.

- Do you drink? (Probably the best answer is, "Occasionally, I'll take a drink.")
- What is the state of your health? (Frankly, this question is illegal. The only question about health or disability that can be asked: Do you have any impairments, physical, mental or medical, which would interfere with your ability to perform the job for which you've applied? They can also legally ask: Are there any job duties that you can't perform because of a physical, mental or medical disability? If so, please describe.)
- If you were starting your career now, what would you do differently? (This one is dangerous because it may bring out that you really don't like the kind of work for which you're applying!)
- Tell me, would you lie for the company? (Hedge on this one. The best response——I'd do nothing to hurt the company.)
- What is your philosophy of life? Of business?
- What is your net worth? (This is a valid question to ask of a financial person. It probably isn't any of their business if you're looking for something else.)
- How much salary do you expect to get? What are your salary requirements? How much money are you asking? (On dealing with the salary question, see the section at the end of this chapter.)

Some other questions you should be ready to answer and may be asked:

- In your capacity as a —— at the X company, what did you actually do? Tell me in detail.
- What kind of work do you think you might be expected to do if you come to work for us?
- If you've done work along these lines, what in your experience would fit you for this job? (Interviewers frequently tell applicants about the job, then ask this question. They're expecting you to summarize your background and experience and relate it to the position. If you're asked this question, you have a golden opportunity to sell yourself.)
- Are you generally lucky? The interviewer who asks this might

be looking for malcontents or someone who's frustrated. If you answer, "Yes," explain further. Be upbeat——explain how and with what you've been lucky.

- How do you spend your spare time? What are your hobbies? (Shows width of interests.)
- What type of position are you most interested in and would you most like to have? This one's all right if what you want is on the career ladder from the position you're applying for, but be careful. Your answer might be threatening to the interviewer.
- Would you mind discussing any long—term plans that you have for yourself or your family?
- What do people criticize you for? (This question presents the same problem as the question on your strengths and weaknesses. The interviewer is trying to get you to incriminate yourself.) This and the next question are used to bring out your personality traits.
- What do you think are your best qualities?
- Why do you think you'd be good in this job? (The interviewer really wants to know what qualities you have that might especially fit you for the position. But he or she might also be trying to determine if you're a braggart.)
- What is the most difficult thing you've ever tackled? What did you do that was most satisfying? What work was the most monotonous? The answer to these questions show the interviewer the level of your aspirations and your ability to handle detail without being bored to tears.
- Are you a leader? Do you like to be in a leadership position? If so, why? (Being a leader is not the same as managing. The interviewer may be trying to determine your aggressive tendencies.)
- What suggestions did you make in your last job to cut costs, increase profits, improve morale, increase output (or whatever is appropriate to the situation)? What results did you get, and how did you go about getting them? What accomplishments were you proudest of?
- What sort of progress would you expect to be normal in our company?
- What would you like to have done more of on your last job?

□ How did your previous employers treat you? This is another version of Challenger's question, "Tell me about your current and previous employers." Watch your answer carefully. So far as you're concerned, your other employers treated you fine.

□ How does this job compare with others you've applied for? The interviewer may want to know how much shopping around you've done and what your "luck" was. This is really an unfair question, but should be answered by saying something like, "I can't answer that question comparatively. This job is the only one like it I've applied for."

□ We all know that family members tend to be critical of each other. What do your family members criticize you for?

The preceding questions are general and could be used in interviews with applicants for almost any job. You may be asked questions to elicit more details about the information, achievements, job responsibilities and duties you listed on your resumé.

Of course, you'll be asked strictly job—related questions. A person applying for a sales position, for example, might be asked questions such as:

□ What kind of products and services have you sold before?

□ What were your typical customers like?

□ How would you go about selling our products (or services) to a typical customer?

□ Which type of selling gives you greater satisfaction, frequent small successes or many turndowns followed by a big success?

□ Do you think selling requires better health than inside work?

The ground is safer on job—related questions. You can answer the questions in a straightforward manner, without feeling trapped in a quagmire. But be careful here. Answer the questions according to your analysis of your interviewer. If you perceive the interviewer to be a High D or High I, use a broad brush in your responses. Offer detail only if the interviewer asks for more. With a High S or High C, respond fully and in detail from the beginning. A High S or High C would consider a broad brush response to be dissembling.

Questions You Should Ask
During the various interviews, you need to gather enough information to allow yourself to make a considered judgment about whether to accept the position or not. Some of these answers you can get from other information sources. And some of the information may have no particular relevance for you. Prepare your list of questions, then take it along with you to use as a prompt sheet or notes. Some of the questions you might ask:

1. Questions about the company:

    What products does it manufacture, or what services does it provide?

    How does the company market its products or services? Direct, through dealers, wholesalers, manufacturer's agents?

    What position does the company have in the industry? Is it the market leader, in the middle of the pack, or does it have to market on price alone?

    What are the sales figures? What is the growth pattern? (Ask for the annual sales volume for the past five years to get an idea of the trends.) What is the overall profitability of the company?

    What problems does the company face?

    What are the strengths and weaknesses of the company?

    Is the company publicly or privately owned? If privately owned, who owns it, and what positions do other family members have in the organization? (This is especially important in family—owned firms. There may truly be no room for growth for an outsider.)

    What companies are the major competitors? How strong are they as competitors? What are their strengths and weaknesses.

2. Questions about your duties and responsibilities:

    What is the job title? Is there a job description? Could you see it? What are the duties and responsibilities of the position?

    What are the reporting relationships? Who does the job report to, and what positions and how many people report to it?

    What kind of authority does the position have? Does it have hiring, firing and training authority? Budgeting and purchasing authority? What decisions can you make without getting higher management or committee approvals?

    What does management hope you would accomplish in this position? What goals and objectives do they have in mind?

3. Questions about your department:

    What is the current status of the department? Does management consider that it's well run and efficient, or is it a department in trouble and they're looking for someone to revamp it?

    What does management expect the department to do? What is its purpose, its place in the overall organization?

    What is different about this department that sets it apart from other similar departments? Any special patents, processes, programs, procedures?

    What size is the budget? How is the budget determined and how much control would you have over it?

    What about the department personnel? What are the overall strengths and weaknesses of the people? (You're not looking for a dossier on individuals, just an overall assessment.)

What are the weak spots in the department? The strengths? What changes does management feel should be made? How soon would they expect them to be made? Would you be able to plan and implement the changes yourself or would they be imposed from above?

What is the structure of the department?

What kind of department records are available? How is the performance of the department and of department personnel evaluated? What about productivity, cost control, efficiency?

What kind of planning does the department currently do, and what planning is expected in the future?

Why do they want to hire someone from the outside rather than promote from within? Could this cause a problem with department employees?

4. Questions about the professional or technical aspects of the position.

These questions you'll have to prepare yourself. They will be job specific. For instance, if you're looking for a research chemist position, you'd have a number of questions about the laboratory facilities, the testing equipment you'd have available, the processes you'd be working with, the budget, the number of patents the laboratory has been granted and who owns them, etc. A teacher or professor would be interested in teaching load, class assignments, the character of the student body, etc. A salesman would be interested in the territory, the way expenses are handled, the training, the commission rate, and so on.

5. Questions about compensation and perquisites.

Don't go into these until you've been made an offer and are seriously considering the position.

What is the salary range? Are there any bonus or stock options? Is any part of the compensation package tied to performance?

What kind of benefits are available? Medical, hospitalization, dental plan, life insurance, salary continuance, etc.

Is there a retirement program? When is it vested? Is it contributory or noncontributory? Can you increase your pension contribution either through a savings program or a deferred compensation program? Are there any other special savings or pension options?

Will you be asked to sign an employment contract? If so, what are its terms? (Not many contracts are being given currently, but you may be asked to sign noncompete agreements or agreements related to company secrets.)

6.   Questions about relocation (only if you'd have to move).

What moving expenses are paid? Does this include packing as well as shipping expenses (you won't have to do any of it or pay for any of it yourself)?

Will they pay for a trip by your spouse to look over the community and for housing?

When would they like you to begin work? Will they give you enough time to make home arrangements and help supervise the packing and moving?

What kind of per diem arrangements will you have during the move? Does it include personal expenses for the entire family while you stay in a hotel or motel during the move?

If the move is delayed for any reason, will the company provide transportation for you to visit your family regularly until all the arrangements can be completed?

7.   Questions to ask yourself during the interview(s) before you make a final decision.

Do you like the people you've met? Do you think you can work with them? Consider superiors, peers and those you met who would be reporting to you.

Can you do the job? Would the job be interesting and provide the challenge you'd like? (Or would you be bored with it after a while?) What would you have to work hard at? What additional skills would you have to get on the job? Are provisions available that will help you get those skills?

Is the company well run? What's your opinion of the management you've met? Would they support you enough to enable you to do what they'd expect you to do?

Do you like and agree with what the organization does as a business?

What kind of pressures would you have? Would you be able to cope with them?

Illegal Questions

Recent employment laws have made certain questions illegal. The Equal Employment Opportunities Act restricted questions that could be asked of members of minority groups and women. Then later laws restricted questions about age, health and physical disabilities. Briefly stated, the restrictions on questions that can be asked and on the topics that can be discussed prior to employment:

Topics that can't be asked about, for or discussed in any form:

1. Race or color
2. Religion or creed
3. National origin
4. Sex (male, female)
5. Marital status

6. Birth control
7. Age (other than if the applicant is between 18 and 70)
8. Birthplace

9. Birth date (this and the question on marital status can be asked after you're employed)
10. Photograph

11. Who to notify in case of an emergency (this question can be asked after you've been employed).

Topics with restrictions:

Topic	Can ask	Can't ask
1. Name	Have you ever worked for this company under another name? Will we need any other information such as a change of name or use of a nickname to check on your work record?	What is your maiden name? Have you ever worked under another name?
2. Criminal or arrest	Have you ever been convicted of a crime? If so, give details.	Have you ever been arrested?
3. Physical, mental or medical disability	Do you have any impairment that might interfere with your ability to perform the job? Is there any type of position you can't hold or job duties you can't perform because of a physical, mental or medical disability? If so, describe.	What diseases have you had? What disabilities do you have?
4. Citizenship	Are you a citizen or do you intend to become one?	When were you naturalized? Are your parents or is your spouse naturalized or native born?
5. Languages	What languages can you speak?	What was your native language? Where did you learn to read and speak the languages you know?
6. Relatives	What relatives other than your spouse are presently employed by our company?	What are the names, addresses or other information about spouse, children, parents, or other relatives not employed by this company? Any question about a spouse.

| 7. | Military | In what branch of the U.S. Armed Forces or (state) militia have you served? | Any question about general military experience. |
| 8. | Memberships | To what professional organizations related to this kind of work do you belong? | To what clubs, societies, or lodges do you belong? |

Topics that can be discussed in detail:

1. Education What schools, colleges and so on did you attend? What are their names and locations? When did you attend? When did you graduate? What other specialized training or courses related to work have you taken?

2. Work experience Where have you worked? When did you work there? What was your position and what work did you do?[1]

Dealing with the Salary Question

You don't want to get into the salary question early in the interview. You want an opportunity to make several Needs/Benefits Link-Up Statements that show your qualifications first. A good time to deal with the salary question is sometime toward the end of the first interview, although the question can be held until a second or third interview if the rest of the interview is going well. If the interviewer appears to be rushing into the salary discussion before you know enough about the position or have had an adequate opportunity to present your qualifications, you can stall the discussion for a while by saying something like:

It would be easier for me to discuss my salary needs if I understood more about the job and how my qualifications might fit it. Could we discuss the job in more detail?

I would expect a salary that's commensurate with my experience and is appropriate to the duties and responsibilities of the job.

I imagine that the company has already established a salary range for that position. What did you have in mind?

---

1. E. Patricia Birsner and Ronald D. Balsley, *Practical Guide to Customer Service Management and Operations*, New York: AMACOM, 1982, pp. 54-55.

You should have a figure in mind that's a minimum you'd accept. Generally, that would be somewhere between 10 and 20 percent more than you got in your previous position. Don't let the interviewer maneuver you into a box where you state a salary that's too low for the position or that's tied to what you made on your last job.

If, on the other hand, the interviewer appears to be stalling on the salary question, you may be spinning your wheels on the interview. Try a tactical question or even an Interview Conclusion Statement to find out where you stand.

Dealing with Difficult Questions about Career Problems

How do you handle those really tough questions when you've had some problems during your career? The toughest areas to handle:

1. You had trouble on your last job(s) and know you'll have one or more poor references.
2. You've been unemployed for a long period of time.
3. You've had a number of jobs recently. You've either been job-hopping or you've had trouble handling the job and have been let go.
4. You're overqualified for the position for which you're applying.

You can't minimize the problems. They're real and the interviewer's concerns have to be addressed. Essentially, you can handle these problems in three ways: 1) you can waste a lot of time trying to justify yourself (usually an unproductive approach); 2) you may refuse to discuss the problem in a vain hope that if you don't talk about it, the problem will "go away" (also usually unproductive); or 3) you can try to get some kind of benefit from the situation that will be an advantage to an employer. In other words, try to turn a weakness into a strength.

A long period of unemployment might be turned to advantage by pointing out that you'd used that time period to learn new skills and update existing ones. The age question might be turned around by pointing out that as a more mature person, you're more stable and would be less likely to job hop than would a younger person.

If you don't want to be questioned about a problem area or areas in an interview, you can make book on it that the interviewer will question you about it or them. Whatever the problem, meet it head on. Don't try to evade the question, remain silent, exhibit fear or become angry. Those are the questions to practice answering with family members or friends until you come up with a response that will put you in the most favorable light (without lying), yet honestly answer the interviewer's question.

Dealing with Questions Related to Age

Another batch of really tough questions relate directly or indirectly to your age. They are tough to answer, and you have to prepare some kind of response in advance.

In the first, you are asked questions about your profession or career area to determine whether or not you've kept your skills up-to-date. (The prospective employer is afraid that your skills are obsolete.) The easiest answer to this kind of question is to be able to respond that you've kept current by taking seminars, self-study, or by keeping your department at the state-of-the-art. If, however, you've been managing people and haven't stayed current, you'll have a different response. You say that on your most recent job assignment, you managed people (or planned, or whatever). In essence, you made a career change and haven't been working at your original profession. You could expand further upon this thought by saying that you could certainly manage professionals in that area, though.

As you already know, you can't be asked directly how old you are. But if the potential employer *thinks* you're too old or has a general prejudice against hiring older employees, you may be asked questions that skirt the topic. Many employers still work on the false assumption that older executives have reduced capabilities. Point out that some of the world's sharpest business people are old. Older executives also have fewer distractions than younger executives, they have maturity and judgment, they've learned to focus on the job at hand and have positive experiences they can use as guidance. The best way to get around this whole area is to present an appearance that negates the stereotypes of age. Then the interviewer is less likely to even consider age as a deselector.

Pension

The employer is worried about providing your pension. You won't have enough time to provide an adequate "cushion" of covered work. Currently, only about one-third of the workers in any company stay there long enough to be vested in the company's pension plan. Also, most pension plans make payouts that are proportional to the number of years an individual has worked and been covered under the plan. You might ask the interviewer to calculate the cost of the pension to the company in comparison to someone making a comparable salary, but working there for more years. But many companies are also turning to alternative methods of financing their pensions. For example, IRAs now can be made a part of a company's pension plan. Both you and the company contribute to IRAs specifically purchased on your behalf. Then, should you leave the company early, you still have the IRAs. Some companies also have deferred compensation plans for older executives which have been worked out to take care of some of the pension problems involved with hiring older workers. (They're also a good deal for the companies and for younger workers who have been job-hopping.)

Practice in Advance—the Mock Interview

Too many applicants talk too much during the interview. They're so uncomfortable that if there are even a few moments of silence, they jump in and fill the silence with words. They offer too much information—they don't choose carefully enough what they tell the interviewer. And, they don't get enough information about the position to be able to make a valid judgment.

How do you become better at interviewing? You plan for different types of interviews, then you practice them with friends, relatives or other job hunters. Start with this technique:

1. Read through the list of questions that you should be able to

answer in this chapter. Choose 15 to 20 that would be representative—include at least two of the bad ones you hope you won't be asked—and organize them on a "crib" sheet.

2. Use the list to prepare yourself for interviews. Read each question to yourself, then formulate what you think would be an appropriate response to make to a High D interviewer. After you've completed the questions for the High D, go through the complete process again for each of the other three communications styles.

3. Ask someone to help you by acting as an interviewer. Explain that you'd like to practice responding to different kinds of interviewers, and ask them if they're willing to role-play with you. Tell them a little about the way a person who's communicating in a High D style would behave, then ask them to conduct a mock interview using the questions on the crib sheet. You're not trying for a complete interview, just the part where you're called on to respond to information-gathering questions.

4. Go through the question-and-answer procedure for the High D. Listen for feedback on the effect your answers are having. If you think you've fouled up an answer, ask to try it again. Record the interview on a tape recorder.

5. After you've gone through the questions, ask the mock interviewer for feedback. What answers were good, which need work, how did you handle the tough ones, what suggestions do they have to make? Work together to develop better answers on the responses that weren't so good. Listen to the tape, if you need to locate exact responses. (You may choose to listen to the answers alone later, if you're restricted on time.)

6. Repeat the interview in High I style, then High S and High C.

After you feel you have your question responses firmly in hand, practice a more free-flowing interview. In this one, you begin with a newspaper advertisement for a position in which you're interested. You glean as much information about the job and the company as you can from the advertisement and from the information sources that are readily available to you. Give the ad to your mock interviewer and ask him to interview you as though he were hiring for the position in the ad. He can act in any style he wishes—or just be himself. At any rate, go through the interview process, making it as lifelike as possible. Record the session, for later playback and review.

What to look for in the critique and playback:

Were you responsive to the clues and cues you got from the interviewer?

Were the answers clear and convincing? Did they give the interviewer a positive picture of you?

What about your voice tone and inflection? Did you show stress in your voice or did you hesitate or stumble unduly when you responded to the difficult questions?

Were you stepping on the interviewer's lines—talking too much, or not giving him or her enough time to react?

Did you understand correctly what the interviewer said to you and make an appropriate response?

Did you remember to paraphrase and summarize? To use Strategic and Tactical questions?

After each real interview, you should similarly "debrief" yourself. Were you able to evaluate the communications style of the interviewer? Did you feel that most of your responses were on target? What questions should you have answered better? Work on adequate responses. Write them down and practice saying them. What did you do especially well? Were you nervous or did you have any other physical or emotional discomfort? Did you feel as though you were paying enough attention to the interviewer, or were you too aware of the way you were feeling, of thinking too much about your next response?

If you can apply even half of what you've learned in this book and add that to your own good judgment and ability, you'll be an interview pro—who gets the job.

Part 4

Evaluating the Job Offer, Making the Decision, and Beginning Work

Evaluating the Job Offer, Making the Decision, and Beginning Work

Almost the worst part of being unemployed is being on tenterhooks after you've had one or several interviews that seemed favorable. You want to get back to work. Remaining unemployed is too emotionally draining. But until the job offer is in hand, you can't let down. You must continue to look and not put all your eggs in one basket. How will you deal with the disappointment if the offer you're depending on doesn't materialize? The situation is a little like the favorite saying from vaudeville: "It isn't over until the fat lady sings." And in this instance, the "fat lady" is the job offer and your acceptance.

How can you get the "fat lady" to sing earlier? Let's say you just completed one or several interviews with a company. You haven't received a job offer yet, but you know the interviewer was interested. Can you do anything to push for the offer without seeming pushy? Yes. You have several options, all of which fall in the area of "asking for the job."

Write an enthusiastic letter. Tell the interviewer how impressed you were with the company, and tell him that you're "raring to go." You really want the job and can start in two weeks, next week, or next Monday.

Telephone the interviewer. Have a definite starting date in mind. Say something like, "I'm very impressed with your company and want to go to work for you. I've researched your company thoroughly, and the more I find out, the better I like it. I can start to work for you next Monday. Will that be all right?" If that seems too strong, try ending with something like, "Can you give me your decision now, or should I call back this afternoon?" In both instances, you asked for the job. They can say "yes" or "no." But you'll know. And some interviewers don't hire unless the applicant asks for the job.

If your interview was arranged by an agency, follow-up with the counselor. Ask to talk with the counselor, either in person or on the telephone as a debriefing. Tell him or her the full results of the interview. Then, follow up with the employer yourself.

Another method which gets attention. Send a Western Union Mailgram to the interviewer. It will cost several dollars, but interviewers know that, too, and understand the importance you place on the mailgram. In your 20 words, you could say something like: "Thanks for meeting with me. I like your company. Am ready to go to work. Will call Wednesday to find out when."

You'll know a company is serious when it asks for your references and begins to check them.

Evaluating the Job Offer

An employer (or two or three) makes you a job offer. Before you say, "Fine, I accept and will start immediately," seriously evaluate the firm, the offer, and the match between you and them. Is this job really what you want? Or are you accepting it because you're desperate? Invariably, if you take a job for the latter reason, you'll be back on the street again within a year because you don't fit them, or they don't fit you.

How Well Do You Fit the Job Characteristics? If you can get a job description or a copy of the job requisition from the person who offered you the job, go back to Chapter 5 and make an estimate of the various job characteristics using the Position Concept Form in Figure 5.2. Score the form and compare the profile of the offered job with the profile of the one you said you wanted (Figure 5.3). Also, check the position profile of the job with your own communications style (the public concept profile you completed on Figure 4.5). What problems might you have?

Find out everything you can about the job. Do some additional research on the company. What would your duties be, who would you report to, what is the climate in the company? If you know an employee, ask him some discreet questions about general conditions at the firm. Ask knowledgeable people in the community—bankers, lawyers, stockbrokers—about the company's general reputation. Try to do as much cross-checking as you can. If the answers vary widely, be careful.

Check out what you've learned about the job with what you learned about yourself. Would it require some skills you don't have or require that you upgrade existing skills? Would it play to your weaknesses instead of your strengths? Is it a detail job or a broad picture job? (Which are you—a detail person or a broad picture person?) Would you be working with things or with people? Which do you do best? Do you have the necessary background and experience to do the job well without a long learning period?

Will the Job Give You the Satisfactions You Require? How does each offer you've received stack up against the criteria you developed earlier in your job search? Up to the time of the offer, you were selling yourself. Now, you're being sold to. Don't buy a lemon.

Take the time to really think about the job. Prepare a checklist like the one in Figure 11.1. If an item doesn't apply to the position, delete it. Also add any other criteria that are important to you. Rate each criteria on the basis of 1 to 5. Give a 5 rating if that characteristic of the job is extremely attractive, a 4 if it's attractive, 3 for acceptable, 2 could be better, and a 1 for not acceptable.

After you complete your scoring, go back over the list. Decide which of these factors is especially important to you——would, in fact, be a critical factor. Check your responses on these items. They're deselectors. Have you rated each critical item a four or five? If you have more than one critical factor that's rated three or less, don't accept the position.

When you have several job offers you're considering, you can evaluate them side by side on the chart. Weigh the scores by multiplying each critical factor by five, the factors that aren't very important to you by one, and those with moderate importance by three. Add up the totals for each offer and compare. You'll have a combination quantitative/qualitative measure that will be of more value than just your intuition.

Figure 11.1. Checklist to Evaluate Job Offers

Checklist Items	Position 1			Position 2			Position 3		
	Score (1 to 5)	Critical factor or weight	Total Score	Score (1 to 5)	Critical factor or weight	Total Score	Score (1 to 5)	Critical factor or weight	Total Score
The company:									
Stability									
Reputation									
Quality of products or services									
Competitive position									
Fiscal condition									
Corporate climate									
Quality of management									
The position:									
Relationship to career goals									
Compensation (salary)									
Bonus arrangements									
Benefits									
Perquisites									
Status									
Creativity									
Flexibility									

Autonomy

Variety

Growth potential

Opportunity for advancement

Intellectual challenge

Quality of staff

Quality of co-workers

Social contacts

Meets personal values

Life style

Relocation

Family disruption

Commuting distance

Travel

Time requirements

Community

Other: list

But do keep in mind that the most significant factor of your performance on the job will be your boss. If you have any reservations about this person——does he or she play by the rules, will your personalities clash, do your work styles mesh——think long and hard about accepting the position. You may have been made an offer you can't refuse. But if the chemistry just isn't there, you may not last on the job, or you'll be miserable.

Negotiating Salary and Benefits. When the talk finally gets around to salary, it's time to play hardball. What is the compensation package? Is the salary similar to that made by others in your field with similar titles (is it the going rate)? Where does the offer fit in the company's salary range? Is it negotiable? (At least begin by asking 10 to 15 percent over your last salary level.) Is compensation strictly salary, or can you earn bonuses?

What about the fringe benefits? These are usually fixed, but you should know the benefits the company offers and get some idea of their worth. You also want to know if they're using a cafeteria plan on benefits and what your choices are. Do you get a car, stock options, educational and travel reimbursement, health and dental insurance, an income savings plan? What about the pension plan? At your age, this should be a major concern. When will you be vested? Is there a supplemental pension program? You also must get complete financial information about a move, if you'll have to relocate.

What do you do if the salary is not acceptable? If the offer is interesting otherwise, at least ask for 5 to 10 percent more than they offered originally. If that won't wash, ask when raises are given, and when they make their salary reviews. You might get them to make a trade—off by giving you an earlier than normal review.

Other financial considerations. What is the career path? Do you have an opportunity for rapid advancement with attendant pay increases, or is it a dead—end job? Can you negotiate a termination agreement or an employment contract?

Making the Decision

You have to fish or cut bait. Do you take the job or don't you? If the offer is mediocre and you have other activity going on, you can probably take the risk and turn the offer down.

But if you've been out of work a long time, you'll be tempted to accept. Hold off a few days if you can before you give your final acceptance. You want to be as sure as you can. Don't let your panic about the need to work push you into a rash decision. If you make the wrong decision, you could be back on the streets again in just a few months, feeling worse about yourself then you do right now.

In some fields, your skills will almost always be highly marketable. You may get job offers before you've really had time to look around. You can end up in a trap, and in a job no better than what you left.

Involving Family in Decision. When the job offer requires relocation or a change in life style, working hours, or anything which will impact upon your family life, involve your family in the decision. Discuss the pros and cons of the offer with them, and of the way each of you might be affected. Consider carefully how a change might affect each individual. Are the advantages of the offer worth the upheaval? Or are the opportunities and changes so attractive that everyone looks forward to the move?

Family members can also help when the decision is difficult even when no move is contemplated. Should you hold out longer, are they willing to continue making the sacrifices they've been making? Having an opportunity to be in on the decision is important to family members.

Notifying Interviewing Company of Decision. After you've made your decision, notify each company you were considering and tell them what you've decided to do. If you're turning their offer down, do it tactfully. Tell them that you were impressed with their company and with their offer. You're sorry, but another company's offer was more attractive (or offered you more opportunity for growth, or didn't require that you relocate).

Finally, notify your friends that you're starting work. Thank again the people who helped you with your campaign.

Was There Any Age Discrimination?

What do you do if you didn't get a job that you were fully qualified for and wanted, and you think that age discrimination is the reason why? It's difficult to decide whether you were the victim of age discrimination or not. Fortunately, the climate on age is changing somewhat as employers discover that older employees have some advantages over young employees. Older employees are more reliable, are absent less, have fewer drug— and alcohol—related problems, work steadier with fewer emotional problems, and are less likely to quit.

However, age discrimination still occurs. You can suspect it if any of the following occurs:

□ You pass all of the required qualifying tests and are still refused a job.

□ You don't get an opportunity to take the tests.

□ You take the tests and are sure you did well. You're told that you didn't pass, but are denied proof.

□ Your credentials are more than adequate, but you're told your education is inadequate, or you lack the necessary formal education.

□ You noted during the interview that everyone in the company is under 40. You check around and discover that the firm never hires anyone over 50.

□ You're asked to take a physical exam or some other test that has no relationship to the demands of the job.

□ During the interview, and before you've been made an offer, you're asked how old you are.

□ You unfortunately reveal during the interview that you have a minor handicap, but that it doesn't interfere with your ability to do the job.

□ You mention in passing during the interview that you're a member of AARP, a political action group, the ERA or some other political or religious group.

□ To discourage you from accepting the job, the employer falsely tells you that you won't be covered by their benefit programs because your spouse is covered on his or her job.

Older women executives and professionals run into both age and sex discrimination, although that, too, is better than it was 20 years ago. Women are protected against discrimination by the ADEA,

Title VII of the Civil Rights Act of 1964, Title VII of the Civil Rights Act of 1967, and the Equal Pay Act. And if older women feel they've been discriminated against, they have more advocacy groups that are willing to take up the cudgel on their behalf.

Where to Go for Help if You Think You've Been Discriminated Against. Discuss your situation first with an advocacy group. Don't go to a lawyer and spend your own hard—earned cash. Many counties have a Family Service League which will help. The U.S. Equal Employment Opportunity Commission is willing to give you advice and help, either at their local office in your area, or you can write to the Commission's main office at 2401 E St., NW, Washington, DC 20506.

The Civil Liberties Union has offices all over and can give you help if they think you have a worthy suit. The National Legal Aid and Defender Association can refer you to attorneys who specialize in age and other discrimination suits. The National Employment Law Project also provides attorney referral, as will a local law school. And the American Association of Retired Persons can give help if you happen to be 60 plus.

But whatever you decide to do, remember that you still have a job to get, so continue your search. Your suit just might not be successful.

Getting Off on the Right Foot

Good. You accepted a job (let's hope it was one you wanted) and the starting day has arrived. Regardless of how long you've worked and how many jobs you've held, beginning a new one is stressful. You're going into a new environment and will be working with new people. They don't do things the way you're used to doing them, and vice versa. You're bound to have mixed emotions. You're excited because you have a new job, but also anxious because you want to do your best——and you want to keep the job.

When you accept a job, you go into partnership with your new employer. You agree to do a job for them, and they agree to pay you for your services. It's to both of your advantages to work out the job details as quickly as possible so that you can get on with it.

Focus on Asking and Learning. Your first few days on the job, you should focus on asking questions of your boss, your co—workers and subordinates. In most instances, even if you're the new boss of the whole works, you aren't expected, and frankly shouldn't, take over and begin to completely revamp operations on the first day. There's too much danger that you'll end up throwing out the baby with the wash water. Regardless of what you were told when you were hired, most of the employees are probably competent and trying to do their jobs. The first few weeks, find out what they are doing, observe who's doing it well, find out as much as you can. Assume the learner's role, and let department employees know you appreciate their help.

Investigate and Ask about Duties and Responsibilities. If your new employer doesn't make arrangements for your training, you'll have to take the bull by the horns yourself. Introduce yourself around. Ask if anyone else has essentially the same kind of job. If so, ask them to describe their job and how they approach their work. Ask them to show you how they do some of the specific tasks.

Ask if there are written job descriptions, any training manuals or handbooks, catalogs of the company's products or services. Read everything about the company and the department that you can get your hands on. Find out what the department's existing goals and objectives are and its purpose for the company.

Determine Formal and Informal Power Structures. A first order of business is to find out about the reporting relationships in your department or division. Who reports to whom, how is the department or division organized? What does the organizational chart look like? Get a copy of the company policies and procedures, if one is available. In major companies, you'll be given an orientation session, a booklet or employee handbook describing the company, the benefits programs and the basic corporate personnel policies. But you also need to understand what the policies and procedures are relative to your job——the department or division policies. If the company doesn't have these policies and procedures in writing, ask to discuss them with your immediate superior so that you won't make mistakes. Then take complete notes to use as a reference.

In addition to the formal power structure, there's an informal social structure in every company that wields a good amount of power. What are the social norms of the department? Who's friends with whom? What about coffee breaks, lunches, general socializing? Make an effort to be friendly, to become acquainted. It's tough to ease into a group. You don't want to be considered standoffish, but neither do you want to blunder. The best way to begin is to observe carefully. With whom do you seem to have rapport? Which people appear to be key members of the department?

Notice who talks with whom, who appear to be the advice givers and the advice takers. Meetings are an excellent opportunity to get a feel for these arrangements. Who sits with whom, who speaks up and commands attention, who speaks up and gets the groans? Unless you're in charge of the meeting, you're better off observing the first few times before you begin to speak out.

Managing Your New Employees

It's a truism that you've been aware of for a long time: Managers don't *motivate* employees; they simply create a good working climate where employees can motivate themselves. As the new executive, you've got to get out of the blocks fast and create that kind of environment.

The same techniques you used earlier to identify and match the communication style of an interviewer will also work in managing employees and in interacting with your superiors and peers. A little more information, though, is in order. Let's relook at each basic style, first for ways that you can manage and encourage people who are communicating in each style, then second, to look at your own personal style as a manager. (Remember: in an unfavorable situation, people may react one way, yet react another way when the environment is favorable.)

Suggestions for Encouraging and Managing

High D   People communicating with this style are active in antagonistic, unfavorable situations. Basically, they like to be challenged, and that's the key to managing them. Give them tough assignments and heavy workloads that force them to extend themselves. Let them compete with others. Put them under pressure.

High Ds work best when they are managed in a direct, straight—forward manner. They need to be able to level with their manager and negotiate on a person—to—person basis. They want and expect to have freedom and authority, power, opportunities to grow, a variety of activities and functions, chances to innovate and material rewards for their work.

High Ds need to learn that empathy for others is not a weakness, it's OK for them to relax, they need some controls, and everyone (even them) has a boss.

High I   People communicating in this style are active in favorable situations. The key to motivating them is recognition. Give them credit within the company and outside it, too, if that's possible. Give them status symbols (nameplates, titles, etc.) that will make them feel important. Give them a chance to speak and to be heard.

High Is work best for democratic managers who are as much their friends as their bosses and with whom they can associate outside of business. They need to have assignments that allow them to interact with and motivate other people. They want and expect to have popularity, prestige and a title, friendly relationships with both their bosses and their peers, favorable working conditions, much interaction with other people and participation in group activities.

High Is need to learn to control their time, meet

deadlines (they often don't really believe deadlines are critical), and manage their money and budgets. They also tend to be far too optimistic, and need to learn to make more realistic assessments of time and people requirements.

High S

People communicating in this style remain passive in favorable situations. To encourage them, show them that you appreciate them, but do it in a low key way. They'd die of embarrassment if you pointed out their achievements in a large meeting. Instead, tell them how you appreciate what they've been doing in the privacy of their offices (or yours). Give them a secure, familiar environment.

Don't upset them with rapid change, if you can avoid it. Prepare them in advance, and give them time to learn. They're so anxious to please that they may need frequent instruction and reassurance at the beginning. But once they're sure of what they're supposed to do, they'll do it well and without further attention. They're happiest with specialized, repetitive work that they can do at their own pace.

High Ss work best for relaxed, amiable managers who take the time to be interested in them as much for themselves as for their work. They want to work for friends. If they like you, they'll work long and hard. But if you push them too much, they can be stubborn and rigid and cause problems. In their work, they expect and want appreciation, sincerity, specialization, limited or no travel, no upsets (they like the status quo), and standard procedures which they can follow.

High Ss need to learn that they get reassurance only when they get results, that change can provide opportunities, that friendship isn't everything, and even friends may need to be disciplined.

High C

People communicating in this style remain passive in situations they feel are unfavorable. They want to be protected, and that's the key to motivating them. Give them exact job descriptions, detailed explanations, and standard operating procedures. Tell them not only what to do, but how to do it. Give them work which they can do without making errors, where precision is important, and where they can share responsibility with someone else.

High Cs work best for supportive managers who maintain an open—door policy and are available for discussion when there are work—related questions. The managers should give them assignments that require planning and precision in carrying them out. They expect and want reassurance, a safe environment (no undue performance or time pressures), low—key personal attention, limited exposure to risk, no sudden changes, and opportunities to participate in teams.

High Cs need to learn that they can't always receive total support, that they must meet deadlines and their work can't always be perfect, job descriptions don't contain all of the duties of a position, and thorough explanation often isn't required or even desired.

It's your responsibility as a manager to communicate with and manage your employees in a manner that will enable them to be most productive for you. You already discovered what your basic communication strengths and weaknesses are. But you can learn more about how these strengths and weaknesses can work for or against you as a manager. When you're aware of ways you may not meet a particular employee's management needs, you can watch for instances when you'll manage better by modifying your behavior. The following information will also be useful to you in assessing other managers (your own bosses, your peers, and managers who report to you). Possible weaknesses are also looked at in terms of typical managerial tasks: planning, organizing, directing, controlling and developing subordinates.

Examining Managerial Behavior in Terms of Communication Style

High D Managers

Dominant managers demonstrate overt aggressiveness. They're competitive, decisive and quick to take action. They respond positively to challenge and are ready to take on both responsibility and authority. In fact, they may usurp authority if boundaries are not firmly established. High D managers may be "people people" if their back-up style (their second highest score above the 50th percentile on their personal concept profile) is a High I. Or, they may be loners (generally represented on a personal concept profile by no other score above the 50th percentile or a second score in the High C or High S quadrant). Regardless, those with whom High D managers come into contact will feel their impact. These managers frustrate quickly, are impatient with nongoal-directed activities and have a high "bore quotient." (They become bored when things run too smoothly. The challenge is gone.)

High D managers work best for superiors who are talented, thus can be respected. They react positively to openness and honesty, so superiors can and should set the limits of authority clearly, then enforce those limits. (You can't be wishy-washy with High D managers. You'll lose their respect.) The ideal environment: fast track, with challenging, unique assignments, plenty of opportunities to prove themselves and the authority to implement their plans. High D managers generally tend either to move up or move out. They get good results, but expect a thrill-a-minute environment, take risks (which may or may not be acceptable to the rest of management) and become disgruntled if they're held back too tightly.

Probable strengths. They're competitive, results oriented, and can both work under pressure and apply it; they're decisive, direct and straightforward, and move quickly and energetically; they accept responsibility and will take the consequences of their actions; and they have almost a compulsion to be active.

Possible weaknesses

□ *Planning.* They tend to be firefighters, may neglect the long range, work day-to-day, and practice "crisis management" rather than "crisis prevention."

□ *Organizing.* They're not always good listeners—in fact, they're often poor listeners and don't get enough information. They usually "tell" rather than "sell." In giving instructions, they generally want people to "do it their way" because they believe they're right. And, they tend to change their priorities and those of their subordinates on the basis of "gut feeling" instead of on the basis of facts and reasoning.

□ *Directing*. They may be impulsive, frequently fail to consult or share, are not always sensitive to others' feelings and needs, and tend to drive, not lead.

□ *Controlling*. They may be poor delegators, preferring to do things themselves because they have confidence in themselves and not in others. They may be impatient and may instill fear in subordinates and peers. They often fail to introduce preventive controls.

□ *Developing subordinates*. They expect subordinates to develop themselves, believe that experience is the best teacher, prefer solving day-to-day problems in preference to training, and are generally not much concerned with developing their people.

High I Managers

Influential managers demonstrate *verbal* aggressivness. They're outgoing, optimistic and prefer working with people rather than things. They have a natural ease and charm that others generally respond to readily. They have a need for others to like them. They like to be center stage and are good at verbalizing. However, they must be careful or they can be perceived as superficial. Sometimes, High I managers have been known to substitute charm for performance. They prefer things to be nice and to run smoothly, and may abdicate responsibility when they run into personnel problems or difficult-people situations. High I managers tend to believe their impressions rather than facts, so may sacrifice thoroughness for speed and expediency.

High I managers work best for superiors who will allow them to "do their own thing." They like variety and freedom coupled with the opportunity to be impressive. They perform best when under close, but not stifling supervision, with lots of positive feedback. High I managers are better at selling than fact finding, motivating than interpreting and promising rather than meeting exacting deadlines. They need well-defined performance standards, understood deadlines, and monitored checkpoints, even though they'll initially resist these controls. They're especially good at initiating people-oriented projects that require selling, but may not adequately follow-up or follow through without prodding. Listen carefully to High I managers' reasons for not meeting deadlines or accomplishing tasks to separate the true reasons from the rationalizations.

Probable strengths. They're persuasive, optimistic, self-confident, enthusiastic and poised. They are good at motivating others, are easy to meet and are friendly and open with other managers and with their subordinates. They make people feel good about themselves.

Possible weaknesses

□ *Planning.* High I managers may trust people more than facts, underestimate problems and overestimate results, generalize rather than deal with specifics, and are prone to superficial analysis.

□ *Organizing.* High I managers may act before thinking, may overcommunicate, telling subordinates more than they need to or should know; they tend to be too trusting, and they may not retain sufficient control.

□ *Directing.* They tend to put their personal popularity first, so frequently have trouble being tough with people, they may overestimate their persuasive abilities, and may be preoccupied with looking good.

□ *Controlling.* They're too trusting of others, they're not always attentive enough to warning signals, they may abdicate their responsibilities, and they may build in excuses they can use in case "things go wrong."

□ *Developing Subordinates.* They talk a good game, but tend to "wing it" rather than plan to build subordinates' competencies. They may go off on tangents and confuse subordinates by saying one thing and doing another because impromptu actions are easy and fun.

High S Managers   Steady managers demonstrate *passive* aggressiveness. They are usually calm, friendly and low key. They'll work hard, they're well organized, loyal and sincere. They're good team players, especially when they feel appreciated. When they're left out, however, they tend to slow things down and don't exhibit much sense of urgency. They don't get bored managing repetitive, task-oriented work. They're usually well liked, are good at maintaining an open-door policy, and can generally be given complete business and personal information without being judgmental.

High S managers work best for friendly superiors who take genuine interest in them both as workers and persons. They work best when they're allowed to set their own pace in a secure, well-established environment. They don't perform well in fast-changing, disruptive environments because they identify with solidarity. High S managers' patience and natural good listening ability make them good confidants and sounding boards within an organization. They prefer a one-task-at-a-time approach, and frequently drive fast-moving High D managers and associates up the wall.

Probable strengths. They are reliable, patient, good listeners, dependable, well organized, systematic, friendly, and they finish what they start.

Possible weaknesses

□ *Planning*. They may be more task than concept oriented and may have trouble planning in global terms. They prefer a well-defined "things to do today" approach to planning. They may not share enough information with other planners.

□ *Organizing.* They are sometimes possessive and would rather work alone. Or, they may build "fiefdoms" of which they're possessive and protective. They may be slow to respond, and may be seen by others as being too indirect. They prefer a low key, soft sell approach which may make them look to be wishy-washy or not assertive enough.

□ *Controlling.* They believe that time is a great healer, so may not take decisive action soon enough. They're frequently too patient to get results. They may procrastinate, and they tend to stay with the tried and true rather than innovating.

□ *Developing subordinates.* They move slowly. They have the patience to be good trainers, but may not move urgently enough. They tend to be selfish with information, and not pass enough of it on to subordinates.

High C Managers

Compliant managers demonstrate *defensive* aggressiveness. They're accurate, attentive to detail, disciplined and are rarely caught unprepared. High C managers usually are very strict. They normally back their orders and directives with quotes from the rules, policy or higher authorities. They're innately cautious, they prefer to avoid trouble rather than to confront it, and may thus appear to be evasive. Since they're usually good with facts, details and statistics, they prefer to let this solid information do their fighting for them. They're highly sensitive to criticism, while at the same time are very good at finding errors of both omission and commission in the work of others.

High C managers work best for a superior who isn't overly time conscious, pressing for results "yesterday." They want and should have enough lead time to do a complete and thorough job. They manage best in a supportive and reassuring environment, with a personally sincere superior. They're well suited to assignments that require persistence, data collection and interpretation, and people dealings which require technical skills rather than persuasive skills. Regardless of the type of work they're asked to do, they'll be much more productive when what they manage is neatly packaged into a system with well-defined goals, performance objectives, checkpoints and rewards.

Probable strengths. They're precise, attentive to detail, well prepared, can and do anticipate problems, follow through, plan thoroughly, deal with facts, and check and double check both their work and that of those they supervise.

Possible weaknesses

□ *Planning.* They may overplan, and spend too much time on planning and not enough on doing. They may concentrate on the small picture and move too slowly and cautiously.

□ *Organizing*. They may overdo, concentrate too much on the details, and insist that everything must be in written form.

□ *Directing*. They may be too strict, count too much on rules and be too rigid, may stifle their subordinates' initiative, and may be more interested that the form and procedures be followed rather than that the desired results be obtained.

□ *Controlling*. They may be slow to trust others, so may oversupervise, requiring that subordinates check back too frequently. They may never be satisfied. They may insist on too much written documentation.

□ *Developing subordinates*. They may overtrain. They may be too concerned with the long term, so may frustrate impatient subordinates, superiors and peers. They're sometimes reluctant to let something go, they tend to "go it alone" and may build fiefdoms. And, they may miss the real issues by being *too* thorough.

As you get to know other executives and your subordinates better, and have an opportunity to see them in both favorable and unfavorable environments, you will begin to see them as whole people. You'll have a better picture of their total communications style, the highs and lows as well as their strengths and weaknesses. By remaining alert and adjusting only those aspects of your personal and managerial style that will impact most heavily on a particular individual, you'll be able to communicate better and more productively, develop your subordinates better and get the work done, if you are to succeed. You may find it helpful to keep notes about each individual's probable style, to "red flag" potential conflict areas and to plan ways to modify the way you work or manage each.

What Have You Accomplished?

If you got this far in this book, you should be employed in a position that will give you satisfaction, while at the same time providing financial rewards. Let's hope that you haven't just given in and "settled" for work that will just keep you busy.

You have also learned a new set of coping and management skills. And, you should have learned a lot more about yourself through your job search process. Your depression (if you were depressed) should be gone. It usually disappears when you begin working, although you may still experience anxiety from time to time. And much about your life should be in better shape than it was before you became unemployed. Above all, you should feel better about your age. Being an older *employed* executive feels a whole lot better than being an older *unemployed* executive!

Let's review your passage through the book. In the introduction, you learned that you were not the only one who's had to work through feelings of rejection, of being too old, of being depressed and having difficulty beginning a search for a new job. Hopefully, this helped you to understand that these feelings are universal and you aren't a loser or abnormal because you felt that way.

In Part I, you began to develop a personal action plan. Not too surprisingly, Chapter 1 provided suggestions to help you cope with all the emotional traumas of being an unemployed older executive (with all the differences that has from being an unemployed younger executive). In Chapter 2, you began putting the various other aspects of your life in order so that you wouldn't be distracted from the larger goal of getting a new job, and also so you would be able to present yourself to potential employers in the best possible light. You also started planning an organized regime in which you approached your job search as a problem-solving activity. Chapter 3 guided you as you began to introspectively evaluate yourself. It should also have helped you search out and organize contacts that could prove useful during the various phases of your job search.

Part II helped you continue and complete your self-evaluation. You learned what your communication style is, and how to make it work for you. You determined your personal level of stress, as well as some ways that you might relieve that stress. Then you continued by investigating in detail the kind of job you should look for, and what kind of personal adaptations you might have to make to satisfy the requirements of that career.

In Part III, you reviewed the basic job search skills—locating possible jobs in both the visible and invisible market, how to write the various kinds of selling resumés (the achievement, chronological, functional and letter), how to remove age from your letters and present yourself as being up-to-date, competent and a valuable potential hire and how to present yourself well, and to understand and use a series of oral communication skills during interviews with potential employers.

This section (Part IV) should have helped you to evaluate and decide upon which job offer to accept. And, just possibly, you received some useful suggestions about beginning your new position so that you could avoid some of the problems you may have encountered on earlier jobs. You also took another look at your own communication style as it relates to managing. By adapting your style as you manage your subordinates and interact with other managers, you should be both more effective and more productive.

With what you already brought to the job search process and what you've learned, you should have all the tools and knowledge you need to be successful.

The Forty Plus Clubs are nonprofit, member-operated cooperatives, dedicated to helping unemployed managers, executives and professionals, forty years of age or older, to conduct an effective job search campaign. Forty Plus has strict entrance requirements since it also functions as a quasi-executive recruitment organization, and wants to assure potential "clients" that the members it recommends for positions have a high standard of excellence.

During the first few weeks of membership, members are put through an in-depth personal examination of their career skills, record and achievements. They are also asked to define their career goals and objectives. During this phase and while they are writing their resumé, they will be coached by members of a club committee called Job Counseling. After they develop what they believe to be an effective resumé, they present it for review and suggestions for improvement before a Job Jury composed of members with similar backgrounds. During this time, they also receive help in setting up their job campaign and can participate in optional classes (interviewing—including a mock interview, communication skills, etc.).

After members complete their resumés, they're assigned to a committee or given a special assignment to operate the club and help each other. One of the committee tasks is to contact potential employers to locate jobs which club members might fill. The club does not charge placement fees, though, to either club members or employers.

But these are not the main advantages of this kind of club. For most members, the real advantage is in their contacts with other unemployed executives like themselves—and in the benefits they get from helping each other. The club also forces people to look at their real accomplishments—what they did for their company. It helps members in four ways: 1) in writing resumés and cover letters; 2) through access to the club's job bank; 3) through the relationships established with other club members, they get moral support—help with interviews, evaluation and financial problems, and practical support—which is one more aspect of networking activities (club members often forward leads to each other); and 4) because they're expected to work at the club two and one-half days a week, they have some place to go, something to do, and can keep their minds active.

The surroundings are not luxurious. Membership dues plus donations from former members are the clubs' primary sources of financial support, so this is understandable. Still, the clubs have the necessary physical equipment for conducting the job search, including word processors. And as the most important aspect to club membership is that of support, members don't seem to mind.

The addresses of the Forty Plus Clubs and of other organizations that might be useful during your job search follow.

Names and Addresses Where Help May Be Available

Forty Plus Clubs

Forty Plus Club of New York
15 Park Row
New York, NY 10038
(212) 233-6086

Forty Plus of Houston
2903 Richmond Ave., Suite 206
Houston, TX 77006
(713) 529-3841

Forty Plus of Colorado
1330 Fox St.
Denver, CO 80204
(303) 893-4040

Forty Plus of Northern California
1990 Embarcadero St.
Oakland, CA 94606
(415) 534-4154

Forty Plus Job Club of Raleigh
4921 Six Forks Road
Raleigh, NC 27609
(919) 787-7353

Forty Plus of Southern California
3750 W. 6th St., Suite 210
Los Angeles, CA 90020
(213) 388-2301

Forty Plus of Philadelphia
1220 Sansom St.
Phildelphia, PA 19107
(215) 923-2074

Forty Plus of Chicago
53 W. Jackson Blvd.
Chicago, IL 60604
(312) 641-0040

Forty Plus of Hawaii
141 Merchant St.
Honolulu, Oahu, Hawaii 96812
(808) 521-2168

Forty Plus Career Development
Center Ltd.
Templar House
81-87 High Holborn
London WC1V6LS, U.K.
01-242-4875/6

Forty Plus of Washington
Webster House Terrace
1718 P St., NW
Washington, DC 20036
(202) 387-1582

Forty Plus of San Diego
8322 Clairemont Mesa Blvd.,
Suite 213
San Diego, CA 92111
(619) 565-8770

Forty Plus of Winston-Salem
P. O. Box 233
Pfafftown, NC 27040
(919) 924-1804

Other Sources of Assistance

Greater New York Area

Advertising Women of New York,
Inc.
153 E. 57th St.
New York, NY 10022
(212) 593-1950

Senior Citizen Action Line
1 Center St.
Municipal Bldg, 15th Floor North
New York, NY 10007
(212) 669-7670

National Manpower Register,
Inc.
635 Madison Ave.
New York, NY 10022
(212) 421-1840
(Technical fields)

Council for Career Planning
310 Madison Ave., Suite 1301
New York, NY 10012
(212) 687-9490

Catalyst-Library & Career
Planning Development Inc.
14 E. 60th St.
New York, NY 10022
(212) 759-9700

Long Island Professional
Career Counseling, Inc.
303 Old Country Road
Hicksville, NY 11801
(516) 938-9100

Professional Placement Center
485 Fifth Ave., 6th Floor
New York, NY 10017
(212) 599-3880

Other Parts of the United States

National Office of Program
Development, Inc.
#2 Illinois Center
233 N. Michigan Ave., Suite 1407
Chicago, IL 60601
(312) 938-0462

Chart
123 E. Grant St., Suite 900
Minneapolis, MN 55403
(612) 871-9100

Career Resources Inc.
2333 Oak Ave.
Northbrook, IL 60062
(312) 274-3169